What Are They Going To Do, Send Me To Vietnam?

My Recollections of a Time So Long Ago

by Jack C. Stoddard
CW2 USA Ret.

KAY,

WE WALKED THE WALK,
AND TALKED THE TALK!

Jack Stoddard

What Are They Going To Do, Send Me To Vietnam?

ISBN: 0-9678055-0-3

Published by:
Sunrise Mountain Publishing
5397 E. Washington Ave.
Las Vegas, Nevada 89110
702-459-4233

Cover designed by:
Robert Hepler
1-626-286-2420

Printed in the USA by:
Morris Publishing
3212 East Highway 30
Kearney, NE 68847
1-800-650-7888

Dedication

This book is written for and dedicated to my sons Jack, Jon, Chris and Billy.

And for the sons, daughters and parents of all the proud soldiers who served in Vietnam. In many ways, this story is every veteran's story.

Table of Contents

◆ Dedication   iii
◆ Foreword   vi
◆ Acknowledgments   ix
◆ Prologue   x

Section One
Going to the 'Nam-M Company 11th Armored Cavalry Regiment

◆ Hey, Wait A Minute   3
◆ Guarding the Runway   11
◆ What, Me Hurt?   15
◆ Black Virgin Mountain   19
◆ Harry and the Grenade   25
◆ The Day the Music Stopped   33
◆ Give Me Hope   41
◆ The Red Headed Lieutenant   47
◆ Row, Row, Row Your Boat   53

Section Two
My New Unit-Aero Rifle Platoon, Air Cavalry Troop, 11th Armored Cavalry Regiment

◆ Wearing of the Black Beret   61
◆ ARPs, My First Mission   67
◆ Back to Michelin   77
◆ Another Day in the ARPs   83
◆ A Surprise For Charlie   89
◆ Night Ambush   95
◆ Just One of Those Days   105

Section Three
Taking A Break

◆   Home Is Where the Heart Is   115
◆   Little Tid Bits   123
◆   Picture Section   129

Section Four
One More Time-B Company, 1/77th Armored Battalion, 5th Infantry Division

◆   The Cop Gets Canned   141
◆   Our Secret Weapon   147
◆   On Donner, On Blitzen   151
◆   The Road to Nowhere   157
◆   We Just Called Him Chicken   163
◆   The Deuce Takes a Swim   167
◆   Believe It Or Not   177
◆   Khe Sanh-My Last Battle   183
◆   Chris Cordova, My Friend   191
◆   Last Flight Out   195

Section Five
Closing the Doors

◆   Going to See Chris   199
◆   Closing the Door For Frank   207
◆   My Buddy Kenny   211

Foreword

In the twenty-five plus years that have passed since the end of the Vietnam War, very little has transpired that has helped us veterans of that war deal with our shared experience. Thinking back over those years, we returned from Vietnam to a hostile society that seemed to blame us for a bankrupt national strategy, watched as the government of South Vietnam gave up in 1975, ached as we saw the overwhelming support accorded Desert Storm veterans that had been denied us, and were angered when our countrymen elected as president a man who can be accurately characterized as a Vietnam draft dodger. For these and a number of other more personal reasons, many Vietnam veterans struggle to this day to bring closure to that period of their lives when they stepped forward to serve their nation. Jack Stoddard has written a book that will help that healing process.

In choosing the title for his book, the author has picked the perfect expression to capture the essence of his text. First of all, that phrase suggests that this is not a book about the grand strategy of the Vietnam War. Thank God! For those of us who fought in that war, we would agree unanimously that if there ever really was a strategy in Vietnam, it certainly was not grand. Instead, Jack Stoddard titled his book with a phase instantly recognizable by every Vietnam veteran and repeated throughout the Army of that period a thousand times over. It suggests a certain irreverence to authority combined with a dogged determination to get on with the task no matter how dangerous or difficult it may have been. It captures in a phrase the spirit and the common bond shared by soldiers in Vietnam. And it is principally for that audience that Jack Stoddard has written this book.

This book is not about colonels, generals, or politicians. It is about common, everyday soldiers, privates, sergeants, and lieutenants. It is about what it was really like to soldier in Vietnam.

We walk with Jack Stoddard from the day he arrives in the country as a green rookie to the day he departs as a battle-hardened sergeant following his second combat tour. In between, we see the entire Vietnam experience - days of boredom interspersed with moments of sheer terror, miserable weather, lonesomeness - everything from hand grenades to hemorrhoids. Through it all, like a common thread, we see the camaraderie that binds together combat soldiers like no other people on earth. It is that bond that holds men together when times get hard and through Jack Stoddard's eyes, we see just how tough things can get, and how strong those bonds can be.

Every Vietnam veteran who reads this book will agree that Jack Stoddard in his own way and in his own style has done a great service to all of us. He has told it like it was and in doing so has helped us all deal with that long ago experience. We were young men who, at the time, never concerned ourselves with the grand strategy or the politics or whether the war was right or wrong. The war was there and we were there and we were going to accomplish our mission to the best of our ability because that was the best way to stay alive. We were proud of our unit, valued our friendships, and did the best we could to care for our buddies. That is why the losses were so personal and the hurt has continued for so long. Jack Stoddard has captured those emotions perfectly and that is why his book is so important.

Vietnam changed my life just like it did Jack Stoddard's and just like it did every other veteran of the war. In my case, when I graduated from West Point in 1967, I wasn't really sure the Army was for me. A tour in Vietnam with the Blackhorse Regiment changed my view. The war, with its brutally effective way of scraping away the parade field nonsense and focusing on what it took to accomplish the mission, showed me why we have an Army and what that Army must be. The Jack Stoddards of the Blackhorse taught me my business, corrected my mistakes, and convinced me that leading them should be the focus of my life. Jack Stoddard has brought all that back for me as if it happened yesterday. I can vividly see my platoons in M Company and K Troop and my service with the Aero Rifle Platoon, the finest group of men ever put on God's earth. Names like Jack, Rollie Port, Lewis Souder, and Frank Saracino, the faces, the battles, the good times and the bad, all come back. And in that coming back to me through Jack Stoddard, I am more convinced than ever that we as soldiers did the right thing. We went, we fought, we took care of each other and we won our part. We served with honor. The rest of it is somebody else's problem and frankly I don't give a damn what those "somebodies" think. The only opinion that counts with me is what we Vietnam veterans think because we are the ones who paid the price.

I know I speak for every Vietnam veteran when I say, "Thank you, Jack Stoddard, for writing this book. You told it like it was, buddy, and no one can do more than that. It was a great honor to have been your Platoon Leader, and to be your friend."

Allons!

Tom White
Brigadier General (Ret.)
Blackhorse Regiment
Vietnam 1968-1969

Acknowledgments

First I'd like to thank my wife, Sue, for putting up with me during this past year. Even if she did keep telling me that one of us would be taken out of here in a body bag. "Look, honey, we did it!" Next is Paul M. Howey of Five Star Star Publications in Chandler, Arizona for all the editing. Then comes retired Brigadier General Tom White for writing my foreword. You were there for me then and here for me now. Thank you, Tom. And last, but not least, thanks to Lynda, Robert and Bruce for all your help.

Prologue

Every soldier who walks this earth has a story. This is mine, or at least the part of my life when I felt the most alive while at the same time being the closest to death. I was a twenty-two-year-old professional soldier who already had five years' experience under his belt when I arrived in Vietnam in 1968.

As a young sergeant, I embraced the challenges of Vietnam. I put my training to the test from the commander's seat of my trusty fifty-ton M48 tank, the Double Deuce, and while walking on patrol as a squad leader of the elite all volunteer Aero Rifle Platoon of Colonel Patton's 11th Armored Cavalry Regiment.

I developed everlasting bonds of friendship, trust, honor, and hope with my closest buddies who were also proud to be called soldiers. There are no Rambos, dopers, or insane killers in my book; just a group of young soldiers, like myself, who were scared most of the time, but had too much pride to show it. We were too busy taking care of each other and just putting up with the daily crap that goes along with any war. We were just regular guys trying to do the best we could - guys with nicknames like Chopper, Lambie-Pie, Jar, Wheatie, Stick, and Pineapple.

I wrote this book because like a lot of other vets, I couldn't tell my own sons about Vietnam, but I knew that I must. There are thousands of other kids like mine, and parents out there who want only to know what their fathers or sons went through and why they still carry the burden of war with them today. This book offers no political opinions nor is it judgmental of Vietnam or the war. Rather it is a collection of true stories about the exciting, humorous, and sometimes frightening adventures I experienced during my two and a half years of combat. This book tells it like it really was, at least for me.

Section One
Going to the 'Nam-M Company 11th Armored Cavalry Regiment

- Hey Wait A Minute
- Guarding the Runway
- What, Me Hurt?
- Black Virgin Mountain
- Harry and the Grenade
- The Day the Music Stopped
- Give Me Hope
- The Redheaded Lieutenant
- Row, Row, Row Your Boat

Hey Wait a Minute

It was the summer of 1968 and I was a young, twenty-two year-old buck sergeant being sent to Vietnam - a strange, faraway place that few if any knew much about. I had already completed an overseas tour in Korea assigned to a tank company stationed south of the DMZ (demilitarized zone). This was different, but still I didn't feel like I was going to war. Maybe it would have if I had arrived in Vietnam earlier with those troops who came over with their entire units. For the most part, these early forces of soldiers and Marines had taken the long ride across the Pacific on troop ships surrounded by friends. By contrast, I didn't know a single soul on my eighteen-hour flight aboard a chartered civilian jetliner from the states. We were replacements for the earlier troops who had either completed their tours and rotated home or had become a casualty of the war.

Our flight from Travis Air Force Base in California to Tan Son Nhut Air Base in South Vietnam had been uneventful and long. The plane was packed with some 300 officers, non-commissioned officers, and enlisted men with most of the latter being in their teens and early twenties. Even with short stopovers in Hawaii and Guam, eighteen hours was just too long to be crammed in the confines of those narrow seats. Our Class A khakis were badly crumpled and looked as if we had slept in them which, as a matter of fact, we had.

The in-flight food was uninspired, but I don't think anyone was thinking much about food. Nevertheless, I enjoyed the steak dinner that was served by the attractive, mini-skirted flight attendant. I wanted to remember the taste of every bite knowing it might be a long time before I'd enjoy anything that good again. After the plane made its bumpy landing at Tan Son Nhut, which had become one of the world's busiest airports, it seemed like it took forever before we finally stopped and the exit door opened. The bright sunlight filtered its way through the plane along with the hot, humid, sticky air that immediately engulfed us. I remember thinking, *boy, will I*

3

be glad to get out of this plane and outside. Maybe there'll be a nice cool breeze to relieve this awful stuffy feeling!

A little nervous and apprehensive, I said to myself, *Well Jack, the ride's over. There's no going back now!* The guys around me started getting up and gathering their gear. I guess they thought that would somehow make the long line move a little faster.

As I looked out the window, I saw the ground crew pushing a metal loading ramp across the steaming tarmac toward us. I hoped it would take me away from this unbearable feeling inside the cramped plane. By the time my feet hit the bottom of the ramp, I had learned my first lesson in Vietnam: there was no cool breeze. That hot sticky feeling that had smothered me inside the plane surrounded me on the ground, too. Welcome to Vietnam, Jack.

As soon as we deplaned, we were loaded on big blue Air Force buses with wire screens covering the windows to be taken to the 90th Replacement Battalion at Long Binh, about an hour from the air base. The young soldier sitting next to me smiled and asked the driver, "Why all the screens? To keep us from getting out?"

The overworked driver replied matter-of-factly, "No, it's to keep the grenades from coming in."

The soldier's smile quickly disappeared as he turned to me and asked, "He's kidding, right?"

I won't go into great detail about my experiences over the next few days other than to say I have never been in so many small offices and long lines in my life. One for filling out your will, the next to get paid, and another to fill out your life insurance form. This went on for two full days until I was finally given my orders to report to the smaller Corp Replacement Center at Bien Hoa. This was where we would complete our final in-processing before being assigned to permanent units.

All of us FNGs (fucking new guys), that's what we were called, did a lot of talking and nervous joking about what to expect from serving with the 11th Armored Cavalry, the famous Blackhorse regiment. I learned, for example, that the history of the regiment dated back to 1902 and had served meritoriously in Vietnam since 1966 and as such, was entitled to numerous unit decorations and

4

awards. The regiment was made up of three squadrons each consisting of one tank company, one artillery battalion and three troops of armored personnel carriers.

I was excited when I found out someone else in my group would be going to the same company as I was. We talked about where we were from and if we had volunteered or had been drafted. It was interesting and a good way to pass the time. We laughed about how we would probably see each other again on the same plane going home. That never did happen though.

Shortly after we arrived at the smaller processing center at Bien Hoa, we were put through a really cool one-day jungle course. It was filled with booby traps, hidden mines, and all sorts of new things we would find as a life-threatening reality in our very near future. While the instructors did their best to make it enjoyable, they also let us know it was deadly serious business and what we learned today could save our lives tomorrow.

At the end of the second day, we were issued our new Olive Drab Blackhorse shoulder patches and told we would be reporting to our assigned units later that evening. I was assigned to M company which was part of the third squadron. Like a good soldier, I rushed over to the local seamstress, a weathered old Vietnamese lady, and had my new patches sewn on.

It was late when three of us new guys were dropped off at the M company orderly room at nearby Xuan Loc, our base camp and the home of the Blackhorse regiment. A sergeant and two of his men helped us unload our gear. After we had evening chow, they showed us to our temporary bunks. I was exhausted by then.

It was hard adjusting to the constant heat and humidity. Everything in the 'Nam seemed to sweat. The canvas covering our hooch was mildewed and the smell was overwhelming. It was just too hot to sleep. It was like being in a furnace. Even my lungs were burning.

I fell on my canvas cot trying to envision what was ahead for me. If only there was a fan to help push this thick air around. Finally I fell asleep, soaked in sweat with my uniform still on and my empty rifle by my side.

5

Early the next morning, about twenty of us new guys from different companies were taken to the helicopter pad in the middle of the camp. Our individual units were all in the field and we would be going to join them. Different types of choppers were taking off and landing all around us. We were guided to a Chinook, one of the largest. By the time everyone and everything was loaded, there were about thirty troopers and three full pallets of supplies on board.

Of this group, less than a dozen were seasoned troopers. We new guys sure must have looked green next to them. They kind of grinned and asked us how many days. They meant, of course, how many days did we have left to serve in country.

"Three-hundred-and-sixty," I said somewhat embarrassed. They all laughed and one yelled out, "Better you than me, buddy!"

While most of them were younger than I was, they appeared much older in their worn and tattered jungle uniforms. I'd been a tanker for nearly five years and was on my second hitch in the Army. I figured I knew my job as well, if not better, than most guys. But now I was really nervous and felt like a raw recruit all over again.

I peeked into the pilot's compartment to see if by chance my brother-in-law, Captain Ric Dickison, could possibly be flying this bird, but I discovered he wasn't. Just then, the twin rotors starting spinning faster and faster and soon we were flying over what seemed to be a busy city.

Before long, we reached the outskirts of the city that was dotted with rice paddies. I watched in amazement as the huge water buffalo and local farmers worked the green fields of new rice.

Within a matter of minutes, we were flying over what appeared from the air to be peaceful jungle. Being naive, I thought this was just too pretty a place for a war. The edges were a light green as new vegetation tried to reclaim the areas that had been cleared by local farmers for their rice paddies. Then the jungle took on a darker green as the younger trees mixed with the older taller trees forming, in effect, a double canopy jungle.

6

Soon we flew over even darker sections of almost black terrain. Three layers of trees had formed together. At that point, the foliage became so thick it was almost impossible to see through it from the ground or the air. I learned from one of the old-timers that this was called, logically, a triple canopy jungle. It looked so beautiful flying over that I couldn't wait to venture into my new surroundings.

I had been daydreaming, but was jolted back to reality when our chopper started to descend into a small clearing that had once been covered with tall elephant grass. The huge, fifty-ton tanks that formed a large circle around it had smashed it completely flat. The chopper scattered dust and loose grass everywhere as we slowly set down in the middle of nowhere.

As we climbed out of the helicopter, not knowing what to expect, I was sure I'd be facing the enemy! That was not to be. Instead, scared and nervous, we all scattered about like baby chicks. A rather tall first sergeant raised his clenched fist and called out, "All right, you FNGs, assemble on me. On the double!"

We gathered around him and he started calling names and telling us where to report. Finally I heard, "Stoddard, Jack, first platoon, M company," and he pointed to a small group of five tanks one hundred yards away.

Filled with excitement, I grabbed my heavy duffel bag, picked up my new rifle, and took off in the direction of my unit. I tried to look as professional as I could but between the weight of my shiny new flack jacket and my helmet bouncing around like crazy on my head, I wasn't doing a very good job. In fact, reflecting back, I must have looked rather comical to say the least.

I ran, then walked, and finally dragged my gear until I reached the first tank in line. I asked where I was supposed to report and one of the crewmembers who were lounging on the back deck told me to go over to the third tank. As I lugged my gear the short distance to Mike One-Four, the platoon sergeant's tank, I overheard something about FNGs and shiny boots.

Sergeant First Class Edwards greeted me and informed me he was the "main man" as the platoon wouldn't have an officer assigned until next week. He instructed me to put my duffel bag on his tank until he decided where to assign me.

About twenty minutes later, a call came over the radio for the platoon to move out. I quickly climbed aboard Mike One-Four and found a spot to sit between the loader's and commander's hatch. SFC Edwards was yelling over the radio for his men to hurry up and finish loading the supplies that had just arrived on the chopper. In five minutes word came down and the five tanks of the first platoon were on the move.

As we rolled out of the perimeter, all kinds of new thoughts and questions filled my mind. *Were we going to a major battle? Back to base camp? I didn't have any ammunition. When or how would I load my rifle? What am I supposed to look for? Will I be a hero or will I want to hide?* I finally decided to just hold on and keep my mouth shut. I'm sure that's what SFC Edwards would have told me anyway.

As we moved further away from the safety of the perimeter, the loader decided to ride inside the tank. That gave me a little more room to sit and I was then able to hang my feet inside the loader's hatch.

Our column of tanks moved off the narrow open path and started cutting its way through the dense jungle to our left. As we slowly forged our way deeper toward some site still unknown to me, branches and tree limbs hit me. I tried to hold onto a handle in front of the loader's hatch and SFC Edwards glanced over and smiled indicating this was perfectly normal.

The jungle became darker and thicker with every minute that went by. It seemed to me as if it was trying to attack and swallow our tanks. I remember thinking, *how could anybody work all day in this unbearable climate?* It was only the middle of the afternoon and I was already soaked to the skin and physically drained by the heat.

Suddenly, the tentacles of a giant prickly vine leaped out at me! In no time, it was wrapped around my chest and was strangling me in a quiet death grip. My first reaction was to scream as loud as I could. "Wait a minute, wait a minute, I'm being pulled off the

8

tank!" but nobody heard me. SFC Edwards wasn't even looking in my direction and because he was wearing his tanker helmet, he couldn't hear me either.

Fortunately the tank wasn't moving very fast, but the monster vine was still tearing at me, pulling me further off the back of the turret. I yelled again, "Wait a minute!" as my legs flew uncontrollably up in the air past the platoon sergeant. I heard him yell to the driver to stop as I was falling to what I feared was certain death. The tank ground to a halt and with one fell swoop, SFC Edwards cut the huge vine away from me with the largest knife I had ever seen.

This big, burly black sergeant was laughing as he pulled me back on top of the turret. "Welcome to Vietnam, kid. You just met your first wait-a-minute vine," he said. He had just saved my life and he thought it was funny! Boy, did I have a lot of learning to do. However, I hoped there would always be someone around like him to help me through the rough spots.

Our company medic cleaned the blood off me, doused me with some smelly antiseptic ointment and then put bandages all over my wounds. I was to be medivaced to the rear area aid station so the stickers could be removed from around my eyes. Did I ever feel dumb!

With that notable and embarrassing exception, I had survived the first day with my new unit. It really wasn't so bad. In fact it turned out to be pretty good. A lot of the guys came over to check me out and said good things like, "You look pretty bad!" And, "Wow, that wait-a-minute vine sure did a number on you!" We even joked and smoked until the dust-off chopper arrived. I was already beginning to feel like one of the guys. Just think, only 359 days to go!

Guarding the Runway

The tanks of the first platoon of M company were once again back at Xuan Loc. Our whole company had been busy pulling long hours of much needed maintenance due our tanks. It had been three days since the wait-a-minute vine incident and I was still covered with bandages and wearing a black patch over my right eye. My eye didn't hurt much and the patch really annoyed me more than anything else.

Around 2:00 P.M., Sergeant First Class Edwards ran into the motor pool telling us to get our tanks put back together and be ready to move out within three hours. The Tet offensive had started and reports had just reached us that both the North Vietnamese Army and the Viet Cong were seen moving into most of the major cities. I felt both excited and nervous as we hurried to finish loading our personal gear on Mike One-One.

My eye patch was the first thing to go before I climbed into the gunner's seat. Our company was going to be split in half with ten of our tanks going with units to Bien Hoa and the other ten heading into Long Binh. The complete 11th Armored Cavalry Regiment would make the one-hundred kilometer trip in less then eight hours, stopping only once for fuel, before splitting up into our two groups: ours headed for Long Binh and the others for Bien Hoa.

Just outside Long Binh, the ten tanks of M company and the ACAVs (armored cavalry assault vehicles) of I and K troops were split into even smaller groups of one and two vehicles. An MP (military police) jeep lead each group to a different part of the city and to the suspected NVA and VC positions.

As gunner on Lieutenant Jacob's tank, it was my job to act as both the gunner and assistant tank commander. It seemed like the lieutenant was always off doing something. But to tell you the truth, I couldn't wait to finally get my own tank. I felt strange playing the dual roles that were expected of me.

In my particular group, my tank took the lead position as Mike One-Two followed twenty feet behind. Moving through the main streets were no problem, but rolling our huge tanks down the side streets was something else altogether! The rear of the tanks knocked large chunks of bricks from the buildings as we tried to turn the sharp narrow corners. We managed to run over everything that wasn't tied down, too. Tables, chairs, even street lamps were crushed under the tracks as we drove our tanks toward our first target.

The MPs radioed us that just fifty yards down the street was a 51-caliber machine gun nest hidden in the bell tower of an old French church. As our two tanks slowly approached, we were hit with a flood of bullets from the suspected target. I raised our 90mm gun tube toward the tower and looked through the sights. I could feel the sweat streaming into my eyes as I waited for the command to fire.

The loader had already inserted an HE (high explosive) round into the main gun tube. The loader sounded off with, "Up!" and Lt. Jacobs yelled out, "Fire!" I responded with, "On the way!" The tank recoiled from the blast and smoke filled the turret as the empty cartridge ejected from the breech.

My first round hit two feet below the machine gun's location and the impact almost cracked the bell tower in half. Huge chunks of white painted cement went flying everywhere with some even landing near our tanks thirty yards away! Within seconds, another round was ready to be fired. This time I aimed it directly at the bell itself. WHAM! the bell and most of the roof disappeared from sight. I watched in excitement and disbelief at the immense firepower of this tank. The once white bell tower was now crumbling. A thin, red line, following a crack, flowed down the side. The upper half of this house of worship no longer existed, it had now become a casualty of the war.

Before we could move to our second target, word came down from higher command for us to get our tanks out of the city. Our tanks were destroying too many buildings maneuvering in the narrow side streets. We were doing more damage than the enemy. Lt. Jacobs was told to have the platoon report to the runway at Tan Son Nhut Air Base and meet up with the rest of M company.

Two hours later, we took up a position at the north end of the runway. Second platoon headed for the south end, almost out of our sight, and another of our platoons took up the position at the main gate. The perimeter at Tan Son Nhut had three security fences spaced about twenty feet apart with sentries walking in between each one. We were positioned inside of the innermost fence, inside the base itself. The dog sentries were removed so we wouldn't hit them if we had to fire our weapons.

The first few days of our new assignment were filled with laying down a good triple barbed wire perimeter between us and the outer walls. The Air Force guys even brought in barrels full of FUGAS (fifty-five gallon drums filled with a mixture of jet and diesel fuels) to be put in front of our first layer of wire. When ignited, these barrels would blow up in a fiery explosion taking out a lot of enemy. We built such a fortress because we were expecting to be attacked by a regiment of NVA. The base had received incoming rockets almost every night, but luckily none had been aimed in our direction. It was hot, sweaty work and we hardly had time to take a break before the next shipment of barbed wire was delivered. All I wanted to do was sleep after these first few days. I didn't even care about the hot showers that were available to us.

Once we had our perimeter set up, our next detail was to sweep the open grassy fields around the runway. We did this twice a day. I liked this because the LT would let me take our tank out and act as tank commander. It was good training for me to get used to working the radios.

On the second day of playing tank commander, everything was going fine until we got about halfway around the huge elephant grass in the outer field. I was in the lead position when all of a sudden WHOOSH! WHOOSH! WHOOSH! Three rockets fired off only five feet in front of the tank. It scared the driver so bad he slammed on the brakes and almost threw me off the tank commander's hatch. Luckily, I grabbed the 50-caliber machine gun handles in the nick of time and didn't fall to the ground. Of course, my eyes were as big as saucers as I watched the trail of smoke from the rockets as they flew toward the main control tower and exploded near the living quarters that surrounded the base of it. I braced myself for the next rocket that I just knew would be heading toward our tank, but it never came. It took us a few minutes to collect ourselves before we started inspecting the area. We found four more well-hidden rockets tied to long bamboo poles that were planted in the soft dirt. They had alarm clocks as timers and it was only a coincident that they had gone off when they had. First thing the following morning, bulldozers were busy cutting down the tall grass!

We had gotten word that a lot of our sister units had already seen some heavy fighting and the NVA did make attempts to attack the base over the next few days, but not in our section. Maybe they were just too scared of our firepower. But let me tell you, we had plenty of sleepless nights.

Even during this major offensive and with our daily job of patrolling the open fields, we found ourselves bored most of the time. I can remember standing next to an Air Force dude watching the large commercial jets load their cargo not more than fifty yards from our perimeter. I watched these strange looking one-man tugs pulling long rows of carts behind them. All of the twenty or so carts had two metal caskets on each of them. I made the mistake of asking my new friend what those little half-sized caskets were for and he just looked at me and said, "Parts man. They're just for parts." Boy did I feel dumb about that one.

There were no bosses or VIPs around, only privates and one sergeant loading these poor soldiers for their last flight home. The respect they showed had no bounds, fore each casket was handled with extreme care. For some strange reason, it made me feel good and a little less worried about dying. At least I knew these fly boys would treat me right.

The tanks of the first platoon stayed on that runway for almost two more weeks of boring days and sleepless nights before word came down that we were to move out and head into the jungle to look for the enemy. They were leaving the cities in droves.

14

What, Me Hurt?

Remember what happened to me with that wait-a-minute vine? Well, I got hurt, again today. Yeah, I know, I've only been in Vietnam for two months. I don't need to worry about the enemy doing me in 'cause I'll do it to myself! Right now I'm sitting in a medevac chopper in agonizing pain. I'll tell you all about it while I'm en route to the evac hospital at our base camp in Xuan Loc.

It was early morning when the five tanks of the first platoon of M company left our NDP (night defensive perimeter) site and headed out on a routine patrol. We had been told to check an approximate two-mile area around our company's position. No big deal, right? About fifteen minutes into our patrol, we had to stop because we came to a deep ravine. The tank commander, Lieutenant Jacobs, decided to cross it on an incline (sideways) instead of head-on which, according to the book, was the way it should have been done. Because of this blunder, the tank threw the left track.

I was pissed to say the least! Even a private knows better than to cross a ravine like that. Now it would take us at least an hour to realign that stubborn track. Ouch! I got so mad thinking about it, I just slammed my hand into the side of the chopper door!

Anyway, two of us climbed off Mike One-One to check the damage. I yelled out to Roberts, our loader, "The track jumped the sprocket. Bring me the tanker bar and let's try to pop it back in place." The tanker bar was a six-foot long metal pry bar and one of the most useful tools onboard the tank.

This next part gets a little tricky to explain. The driver puts the tank in neutral and turns the steering wheel in one direction while accelerating a little. This causes the rear sprocket on one side to rotate forward while the sprocket on the other side stands still. With any luck the jumped track will snap back in place and fall between the large teeth of the sprocket. Lost? There's still one more thing to keep in mind. If for some reason the driver should turn the steering wheel in the wrong direction or doesn't keep giving the tank enough gas, the damaged track will still slam down but instead of falling into place, it will bounce back up causing somebody serious injury.

You guessed it! I was that somebody. As Roberts was giving the hand signals to the lieutenant, I was trying to force the track back on the edge of the sprocket with the tanker bar. Everything went fine at first. Then, unexpectedly, the track jumped up and the bar slipped forcing my left hand between the large teeth of the moving sprocket. The track slammed down against the metal teeth and pinned my hand between the sprocket and the track.

As the track popped up again, I pulled my hand out, fell to the ground and rolled around screaming. Poor Roberts stood there in silent horror. I was in so much pain that I was afraid to look at my hand. I was convinced there was nothing left of it. I thought to myself, *Shit, I'm here only two months and I'm already going home!* The only reason I didn't lose the whole thing was because the track had landed on top of the sprocket teeth and not in between them like it should have.

I ran around in circles yelling every cuss word I had ever known. Some dated back to grade school! By now everyone in the immediate area had come over to see what happened to me. Our platoon medic tried to hold me down so he could check out my injuries. My hand ballooned to at least three times its normal size and turned a deep shade of purple. The medic immediately yelled to Lt. Jacobs, "Get a dust-off in here!" As I sat in the chopper heading for the evac hospital, I was really scared that I would lose my hand.

The pilot just said we're ten minutes out. Damn, if I accidentally hit my hand one more time, I'll let them cut it off! I see the big white cross on the ground. It won't be long now.

The chopper landed on top of the white landing mark and the crew chief directed me to two large canvas curtains that flapped wildly in the wind. I was apprehensive, I was hurt, but I knew I wouldn't die. Besides, I hate doctors and assumed they would do a lot of painful things to me. *This is a no-win situation,* I thought entering the field hospital.

16

The first things I saw were a half-dozen stainless steel tables covered with black rubber mats. It was a scene straight out of an episode of M*A*S*H. There were big lights and poles with plastic bags hanging from them. There were even metal trays on wheels that were filled with stuff I knew I didn't want to know about. It sure was a discomforting sight. I started feeling better immediately.

I saw an Army nurse coming toward me and I attempted to report to her. I started to raise my hand to salute her when she said, "You don't have to do that in here, son. Just let me see your tag." She was referring to my large red medical tag. She read it, looked at my swollen hand, and said they would have to take some x-rays. She told me to take a seat in the meantime. "Don't rush on my account," I remember saying.

So there I was sitting on this wooden bench when a young medic sticks his head in and yells, "Three choppers full on the way!" In an instant, the room was overflowing with doctors and nurses in surgical smocks. I could hear the choppers outside as the medics brought in the wounded men, some of them screaming in pain. A triage doctor directed the medics. Never had I seen so much controlled chaos.

There were six soldiers on the tables and two of the less critically wounded ones on stretchers on the floor. There was a doctor and two nurses at each table. Soldiers' uniforms were being ripped off and IV lines put in their arms. Everyone was yelling for more of this or more of that. One soldier on the far table was getting mouth-to-mouth resuscitation while the one next to him had died. The medics were lowering him to the floor.

I was stunned! So much went on so fast that I couldn't keep up with it all. Within a half-hour the surgeons had lost two soldiers, but the others made it. At least they had made it out of the operating room. The injured were so doped up now they weren't screaming anymore. They were being carried out one at a time into the recovery ward. I don't know about those dedicated doctors and nurses, but I was drained from just watching.

I sat silently on the bench watching an orderly wash away the blood with a hose. I knew then why the tables were covered with rubber. The doctors and nurses had left leaving the medics to clean up the mess. I must have sat there for thirty minutes just watching them. A light touch on my shoulder startled me and I looked up to see the head nurse.

"I'm so sorry, Sgt. Stoddard. You shouldn't have seen that. We should have moved you when the wounded arrived. How is your hand feeling?"

I looked at her and said, "After what I just saw, my hand is feeling great, just great!"

She held my still-throbbing hand and without warning yanked two of my fingers. At once, my hand started to deflate.

"You're lucky," she said smiling. "It was only jammed." She gave me some pain pills and told me to report back to my company.

I felt better as I walked back towards the orderly room. As a matter of fact, after what I just witnessed, it felt good to be alive. I sure never wanted to go back there again, ever.

Instead of going directly back to my company, I stopped off at the NCO (non-commissioned officers) Club and had a beer. Sure, I wasn't supposed to be there, but what are they going to do, send me to Vietnam?

Black Virgin Mountain

I'd been in country for only a short while and was still the gunner on the platoon leader's tank, Mike One-One when my unit was alerted that we would be departing in the morning on a squadron-sized operation. This had to be something big because up until now, all our missions had been smaller, platoon-sized ones. Word was we'd be gone for thirty days, so everyone ran down to the post exchange to load up on goodies. Then we headed for the NCO (non-commissioned officers) Club to get our last good meal for a while.

The worst part about being in base camp were the long lines. No matter where you went, there was always a line. They usually moved pretty fast until some of the guys started doing the "Dap" (a greeting some soldiers did where they would slap hands, elbows, and arms in a series of rhythmic moves). This would go on for anywhere between five and twenty minutes. If new "Dappers" joined in, then it could go on for what seemed like an eternity. At first, this exchange was interesting to watch but it quickly grew tiresome when more and more Dappers joined in and the line in front of you grew longer and longer. Eventually, this custom was curbed by the powers that be because so many soldiers were complaining.

Bright and early the next morning, our tank company, M company, and the rest of the third squadron were on the road. We went south around the outskirts of Saigon and then headed toward the Cambodian border. We stopped the first time for fuel later that morning and by mid-afternoon, I had fallen asleep in the gunner's seat. I still was not adjusted to the torrid climate, plus it was another twenty degrees hotter inside the tank! I felt like I was being baked alive. I awoke when the tank came to a stop and figured we were refueling again. Half asleep but not wanting to get in trouble for not helping, I climbed out the tank commander's hatch. I saw we were deep in the mountains surrounded by a combination of open green fields and thick jungle. We were stopped on a narrow trail just outside of a small village when I saw them.

For a moment, my mind flashed back to when I was a kid at my Grandad's house. I would spend hours sitting in his huge bedroom closet reading and looking at his *National Geographic* magazines. The scene in front of me was just like a picture from one of those issues. A woman with no top on was breast-feeding a baby. Two men standing next to her also had no shirts on. One of them had a crossbow in his hand and arrows strapped to his back. The other guy had a long knife hanging from his belt and both had brightly colored cloth wrapped around their heads.

The tank driver told me these were Montagnards, the primitive hill people of Vietnam, and that they hated the VC and the Vietnamese people, too. He also said to be sure and leave the women alone or they'd kill you. Who'd want them anyway? Besides being old and ugly, they had black teeth and a huge wad of betelenut in their mouths. Still, I found them fascinating. It was like a world within a world. The Montagnards hadn't changed their way of life in hundreds of years. Before long, we were on our way again. Not even this beautiful strange place could stop the progress of the modern day Army on the move.

That evening after we stopped again for fuel and something to eat, we were told that we'd be traveling all night. Roberts, our loader, was driving while our regular driver, Phil, was trying to get some sleep in the gunner's seat. I was now in the loader's position. That was one of the good things about tank crews, we could perform each other's jobs.

All things considered, we were driving at a pretty good clip during the day, but not now. Jungle travel in a tank was never easy, but it was even worse at night with the constant, unseen hazards, especially under blackout driving conditions. Our speed was very slow with only the brightness of a penlight to see by. I still don't know how those drivers ever saw anything!

Around midnight, our large column stopped suddenly. My tank commander, Lieutenant Jacobs, got a call over the radio to send up three tanks with their headlights on ASAP. We were all concerned about this because it broke every rule in the book. With our lights on, we would be a nice target for Charlie.

The ACAVs (armored cavalry assault vehicles or tracks) in front of us had pulled over to the right side of the trail as far as possible allowing our tanks to barely squeeze by. It was slow going but once we had gone about a half-mile up the road, we could see what was going on. Even in the pitch black, I could see a lot of men standing around. An ACAV from I troop had run off the trail into a bomb crater and landed upside down trapping the crew. The driver and track commander were dead and still pinned in the vehicle. The rest of the crew were being crushed by the fifty heavy cans of M60 and 50-caliber ammunition that was normally carried on the floor but was now on top of them. To add to their pain, acid from the vehicle's batteries was leaking all over them. I could hear them screaming over the sound of my own tank as I looked at the tangled mess at the bottom of the huge crater.

Fellow troopers were waiting for us and everyone wanted to help. Tracks were backing up trying to shine their headlights into the deep crater. The I troop commander was desperately trying to take charge and while ground-guiding our tanks into position, he was giving orders to his own men to back off and give us room to work. The smell of battery acid was thick in the air. We had to be very careful not to hurt anyone worse than they already were. The tankers and crews from the ACAVs worked together connecting a long series of tow cables so we could ever so gently turn the ACAV on its side. It took vehicles on both sides, one pushing and one pulling, to accomplish this. We had to be extremely careful because if the track fell too quickly, the fifty boxes of live ammunition could finish crushing a crew member or even worse, the batteries could explode, sending even more acid over them.

Finally after what seemed like a lifetime, we got the ACAV upright and the medics were able to pull the four guys out. Three of them were really messed up from the battery acid. As the medics were cutting off the wounded soldiers' clothes, a medevac chopper landed in a jungle clearing that the tanks of the M company, third platoon had just made. After everything was cleared away and we resumed our mission, we drove with our headlights on. Gooks or no Gooks, our commanders didn't want anything like that to happen again.

At first light, we stopped for a rest. I could see this huge black mountain off in the distance. When I commented about it, the lieutenant told me that's where we were headed. We were told it was called Black Virgin Mountain, but the official name was Nvi-Ba-Den. As far as we knew, this was the first time American troops had attempted to climb it with tanks. It was so tall that the top was shrouded in clouds.

It took us until noon on the second day before we even got to the base of it. We spent the rest of the day setting up a perimeter using tanks and ACAVs in a large circle with the command and medic tracks in the middle. Chinooks dropped in food, water and ammunition all day long. Now we really knew we were getting into something big! All we could do now was try and get some rest.

Early the next morning, because there were only foot trails, we had to cut and smash a road up the mountain by pushing down the thick jungle and rows of bamboo. Of course, the tanks had to take the lead. The job of breaking through the jungle was a miserable one. It took hours to advance only a few hundred yards. It was hot, too. Sticky hot! As we knocked down the jungle, treetops would snap and branches full of bugs would fall on us. Periodically, we had to stop and push the branches off so we wouldn't get eaten alive by the hundreds of small insects. It was just my luck that our tank was second in line.

About a third of the way up, we finally broke into a clearing. Boy, was I glad to get out of that jungle! It looked as if a major bomb strike had gone in because most of the jungle had completely disappeared except for a dozen or so tree stumps. About halfway across the clearing, we came under heavy enemy fire. It started with machine gun and small arms and within ten minutes, all hell broke loose. We had no where to hide. We formed a tight wedge formation as best we could. Each tank was on its own, firing its main guns at the wood line ahead of it. Mike One-Two had bellied himself up on a stump and had taken three direct hits from a barrage of enemy RPGs (rocket-propelled grenades). Within seconds, the tank burst into a massive ball of flames and the crew desperately tried to escape. The NVA (North Vietnamese Army) soldiers were invisible to us as they were well dug into the tree line. All I could hear was confusion over the radio as I looked into my gun sight trying desperately to locate a target, any target.

We continued laying down a combination of 30-caliber and main gun fire. The tank commanders were firing their 50-caliber machine guns. RPG2s and 7s were flying everywhere. You could see them everywhere exploding off tanks, trees, and anything else in their path.

About fifteen minutes into the firefight, the lieutenant told me to leave the gunner's seat and assume the tank commander's position of Mike One-Three on our left flank. The commander had been killed and they now only had a two-man crew. I didn't really want to leave the safety of my own tank, but I knew I had to. I estimated the distance to be about twenty yards and then jumped out through the loader's hatch. I could feel bullets flying past me and saw rockets in the air. You're not going to believe this, but I covered that distance in about three steps and landed on the back deck.

Still shaking, I helped pull the dead sergeant out of the turret and assumed immediate command giving orders to the two scared crew members. Selfishly, I realized if we somehow survived this firefight, I would be a tank commander. A scared silly twenty-two-year-old tank commander.

We continued laying down as much firepower as we could until our artillery started coming in around us. The tanks shook from the impact of large rounds and shrap metal and clods of dirt landed all around. We buttoned up the tanks (closed all the hatches) and put out 30-caliber fire until no more incoming rounds were heard. The battlefield fell silent. It was finally over, for now.

The remaining days of our stay weren't as fierce as the first, just mostly small arm and machine gun fire. We never could see the enemy, but they sure let us know they were still out there. What we didn't know at the time was that this mountain held a labyrinth of tunnels as well as the largest underground hospital in Vietnam and was protected by a division of NVA soldiers.

Just before dark later that day, we finally made it to the top. During the next few days, that's where the ACAVs and infantry soldiers caught hell. They never did find all the tunnel openings.

The weather had turned bad and we were getting heavy two-hour downpours of rain three times a day now. One afternoon, it was raining so hard we couldn't see anything in front of us. Toward the end of the fighting, our tanks were getting bogged down in the thick mud and were essentially useless. All we could do was sit on the top of the mountain.

We had gotten a supply of ammunition and after we were reloaded, my guys went over to the makeshift landing zone to get some hot chow. When they got back, it was my turn so I trudged on over in knee-deep mud and got some dinner. It really wasn't worth the trip. It was raining so hard that all the food was just floating on the paper plate.

I decided not to go all the way back to my tank figuring if I ate the chow now, at least it might still be a little warm. I sat down near the chopper pad on a pile of stuff and started eating. I was tilting my plate so the water could run off at the same time trying not to spill the gravy. While I was eating, people would walk past me and they'd give me a dirty look. I just waved back. I couldn't figure out what was up. I mean at least five people had walked past me and gave me the same funny look. Well. it wasn't long before I was finished eating and when I stood up and turned around, I realized I had been eating dinner on a pile of filled body bags! All I could think of saying was, "Sorry about that guys." I felt really dumb.

Because of the rain, our thirty-day mission was cut down to about ten. As we worked our way down the muddy mountain we were still receiving enemy small arm fire. I wondered if the rest of my tour in 'Nam would be this bad. I know I wasn't the only one who was glad to get out of here. Charlie, you can keep your Black Virgin Mountain!

Harry and the Grenade

I'd only recently assumed command of my new tank - Mike One-Three. The driver was named Harry. I really liked him despite rumors that he smoked a little pot. I have to admit he did look a little strange with his non-regulation long hair, beaded peace symbol hung around his neck, and a driver's compartment he'd painted with unauthorized Day-Glo psychedelic paint. Other than that, he was just like any other member of my crew. One thing was for sure, he could really drive! There was an art to driving a tank through the mountains and jungles of Vietnam and the amount of maintenance required to keep the tanks on the road was enormous. We would have at least two hours of maintenance for every two hours spent driving. Despite his other peculiarities, Harry wasn't afraid of work.

I won't say nobody ever smoked pot in Vietnam, but nobody ever did around me. The dopers, as we called them, would claim that those who drank beer were drunks, then the beer drinkers would go on about how at least they weren't Hippies and getting high all the time. The guys would go round and round never settling anything. They each hung with their own group whenever they were back at base camp. NCOs (non-commissioned officers) lived in their own hooches and hung out with their peers. In a way, we were considered outsiders because it wasn't proper for us to fraternize with the enlisted men while in base camp. That was something I thought was odd since we lived together like brothers in the field, which was where we spent more than ninety percent of our time. But back to my story...

Our unit, the first platoon of M company, had just been given move-out orders. We were to leave Xuan Loc, our base camp, drive through Saigon and then head north to the Cambodian Border. On this particular mission, our five tanks would be under the command of the First Cavalry Division instead of our own unit.

We did this sort of thing all the time. Mostly we'd end up at a small fire support base somewhere waiting to get called into action.

Other times, we'd provide support for the infantry. This was always a lot more interesting work plus time went fast when we were moving through the jungle all day. Our heavy tanks were great in Vietnam, but they had certain limitations on how they could best be used. Many times, the rugged terrain just couldn't support them.

We finally got underway and after a few hours, reached the busy outskirts of Saigon. I clicked on the intercom built into my helmet and said to Harry, "Okay, buddy, let's slow it down a little. We're starting to get into the city."

I'd only been with this crew a few weeks and was still learning their ways. We had been driving non-stop for more than three hours and I wanted to make sure Harry was still alert. It was easy to start daydreaming from the monotony of these long hauls. Strickland, my loader, stuck his head out from inside the turret when we entered the city. He liked "checking out the chicks" as we made our way through the narrow, crowded city streets.

It took about an hour to make it halfway through the city. The afternoon sun was now in my eyes and I hoped this annoying glare would change position soon! About that time, the craziest thing happened. Harry climbed out of the driver's compartment and stood on the front fender of the tank. I thought I was losing it! What the hell was going on? Was I just seeing things? I called him on the intercom, but there was no answer. Then I saw the communication (commo) cord wasn't attached to his helmet.

I climbed out of my cupola and yelled to him, "What in the hell are you doing out there?"

Looking as white as a ghost, he pointed down into the driver's compartment and stammered, "Grenade, grenade! I dropped a grenade and when I tried to pick it up, the pin came out." He showed me the pin that he was holding tightly in his hand.

"Oh shit!" I said as I worked my way to his side. The tank minus its driver had not slowed down and was somehow still moving straight ahead through the crowded city streets. Harry had been driving with the tanker's version of cruise control on.

26

Panicked, I called our platoon leader, "Mike One-One, this is Mike One-Three. We have a live grenade in the turret. Over."

I didn't have much time to talk. I knew what I had to do and had to do it fast. First I had to stop this damn thing before it ran over something or somebody, then I had to find that stupid grenade and disarm it before it exploded and blew us all into a million pieces.

As I continued to chew Harry's ass, I made my way with extreme caution into the darkness of the driver's compartment, being very careful where I put my heavy combat boots. About that same time, I heard our lieutenant calling over the radio.

"Mike One-Three, did you say live grenade? Over."

I felt like saying, *what the fuck did you think I said?* But instead answered back, "Roger, Mike One-One, I have a live grenade in my driver's compartment and I'm looking for it now. Over."

"Mike One-Three, where the hell is your driver? Over."

I disconnected my commo cord as I saw this conversation was going nowhere.

The first thing I did was release the large black knob that locked the gas pedal in one position. By pushing the button in the center and then forcing the whole rod forward, the gas pedal was released and the tank slowed down almost immediately. I was now sitting in the driver's seat, but the gas pedal position didn't feel right to me. *What the hell?* I bent over further, looking everywhere at once for that live grenade.

I finally found it wedged between the inside hull and the backside of the gas pedal. If I hadn't disconnected the cruise control first and forced the pedal up, I probably wouldn't be telling this story. That grenade could have easily shifted causing the handle to fly off and explode in seven seconds. Luckily, the gas pedal helped hold the pin against the hull and I was able to carefully reach down and pick it up while holding the unsecured handle in place.

I slowly guided our tank to the right side of the street with one hand as I held the explosive grenade with the other. I was still yelling at Harry when the tank finally came to a stop. Still shaking, he handed me the grenade pin. This whole crazy ordeal couldn't

27

have taken more than five minutes, but it seemed like an eternity to me!

When I climbed out on the fender, I almost fell off because my legs were shaking so badly. As I looked up toward the tank commander's hatch, I saw both Strickland and Chopper sitting there. I guess I looked as if I was about to ask why they were there when Strickland said, "We may be privates, but we ain't dumb. Chopper and I climbed out of the turret when we heard the word grenade."

He handed me my commo cord and as I hooked it back up I heard, "Mike One-Three, did you say live grenade?! Over."

"It's okay, Mike One-One. We have everything under control, but we've pulled over for a minute." I replied.

"Okay, but quit messing around back there and rejoin the column. Out."

I was now getting a little upset as I got everybody back where they belonged. I informed Harry he was on my shit list and that as soon as we got to our next refueling point, I wanted all of those grenades put away in their proper storage compartments. I never did ask him why he was playing with them. I didn't really care at that point.

When we pulled forward to rejoin the column, I smelled the strong odor of burning rubber. I looked inside the turret and found smoke coming from around the floor. I yelled to my guys to get out of the turret and at the same time told Harry to pull over and shut down the tank. Thick, black smoke along with the intermittent orange color of fire was now leaping out from the rear engine grill doors. *Shit, now what?* I tried to contact Mike One-One. No luck, my radios were dead.

I yelled for Harry to pull the fire extinguisher handles located in his compartment. Instantly, enormous clouds of white smoke and foam covered the rear engine compartment. It was still smoking but I couldn't see flames anymore. *What else could possibly go wrong?* I jumped off the tank and ran into the street to stop Mike One-Five, the last tank in our convoy. Sergeant Whiles, the tank commander, said he would notify Mike One-One for me. Two minutes later, our rear convoy jeep stopped and the driver said that a maintenance truck would be here as soon as possible. I could almost here Lieutenant Jacobs chewing me out. As a matter of fact, I could feel the chunks being taken out.

The four of us stood there in the street, bewildered, looking at our poor smoldering tank. I heard Harry tell Chopper, "Far out, man. Really far out!" I was so mad at Harry that for two cents I'd have killed him!

What came next could only happen in Saigon and to me. I heard at least two sirens coming in our direction and I knew they were headed for us. I didn't even look up. I just thought, *Why not Jack? You might as well enjoy this, it's got to be better than the rest of your day.* Here they came, two small yellow fire trucks with at least fifteen firemen on each of them. It looked like something out of a Keystone Cops movie. They were hanging all over the trucks with their big red fire hats and big black rubber boots on and their yellow jackets blowing all around. I think they took the corner at the end of the block on two wheels. I couldn't help but laugh. The sirens were so loud they hurt my ears. All thirty firemen converged on our tank. Some of them had already started to lay out a giant water hose as others climbed on the tank's rear deck.

There's a right way and wrong way to climb up on a tank. They were doing it the wrong way and were either falling off the side of the tank or slipping on the foam that was still coming out of the engine compartment. The chief fireman was throwing his hands in the air yelling at them in Vietnamese. They looked really upset that our tank wasn't completely engulfed in flames. Soon they were all down on the ground running around putting all their gear away. The chief came up to me and said something, I still don't know what it was, but I told all my guys to thank our friendly firemen and we waved to them as they drove away.

Just when I thought things were getting back to normal, a jeep pulled up with a young second lieutenant and our maintenance NCO onboard. I reported to the lieutenant and we all three talked while we checked out the damage. After twenty minutes or so, it was decided we would have to be towed to our nearest maintenance

29

repair shop at Bien Hoa and that we'd have to wait until morning for the VTR (M88 Vehicle Track Recovery) to get us. I told them we'd be here since we weren't going anywhere, but I don't think they thought that was very funny. At that point, I didn't really care. I had my guys get the tank ready for towing the next day and situated for the night. It took us an hour to unhook everything and put the poncho cover over the tank commander's hatch.

The guys were now tired and thirsty so I decided to take Strickland with me to try and locate some cold beer and Cokes. I left Harry on guard and the two of us took off walking around the block. It didn't take long before we spotted the flashing sign of the Saigon Senior NCO Club. I knew it couldn't be the official NCO Club sitting on this narrow back street of the city, but we went in anyway. It was very small and to my surprise was the real Army club. There were several senior NCOs sitting around the small bar. I asked the bartender if I could buy a case of beer but he said the club was for members only and we would have to leave.

"Okay, dude. I just wanted to get something cold to drink. My tank is broken down and my guys are thirsty." I said.

"Did you say tank?" asked an old first sergeant sitting to my left. He looked over at the worn Blackhorse patch on my left shoulder. Before I could answer him he said, "Give these two guys whatever they want and put it on my tab. I served with the Eleventh my last tour and by god when a tanker is thirsty, he's thirsty!" Now hurry up about it." I thanked him and Strickland and I headed back to our tank with cold cases of both beer and Coke.

As we turned the last corner, I saw Harry standing on top of the tank looking through my binoculars.

"Now what?" I asked Strickland as we hurried to our lonely tank.

"You guys have got to see this!" Harry yelled to us.

"What is it? What's wrong Harry?" I asked as I got closer.

"Nothing's wrong, Sarge. In fact, it's great. Really great!"

I took the binoculars from him and looked in the direction he'd been and I couldn't believe my eyes. There were two young

American girls on the other side of a wall washing a small foreign car. I mean with a bucket of soapy water and all! All I could think was, *Wow!* They were wearing T-shirts and shorts and both of them were very pretty. Of course in the 'Nam, all American girls looked pretty.

By now, Strickland was jumping up and down demanding a turn. Well, you can guess what came next. Yes, after much begging, I let my crew go around the block to find those girls. I figured we were already in so much trouble one more thing wasn't going to matter.

As they headed off down the block I yelled, "I want you guys back here in one hour, you copy? I heard a faint, "Okay, Sarge, okay, no sweat." And with that they were out of sight.

It was getting dark and the few streetlights were now dimly glowing overhead as I saw my guys returning. They had the two girls with them! The two young ladies actually turned out to be French and were attending college while their father worked for the government. They asked if the guys could go to their place and listen to records for a couple more hours. Out of the corner of my eye, I saw Chopper taking the case of beer off the tank.

I couldn't refuse these two lovely girls so I told my guys, "Okay, only two hours and then I expect you back here." I looked at Chopper and added, "And I mean sober, too!" I was only twenty-two, but for some strange reason I felt like a father telling his kids to behave.

My guys showed up on time two hours later. From the way they were talking you'd think they'd just returned from the prom. We did everything by the book for the rest of the night, just as if we were in the field with our tank platoon.

Early the next morning, the VTR arrived and we spent an hour hooking up Mike One-Three behind it. The timing couldn't have been better because as we were pulling out, the two girls came out of their house and waved goodbye. The crew of the VTR cheered and whistled.

A little more than two hours later found us at the front gate of our home for the next eight days, the Bien Hoa Maintenance

Support Company. We were told the complete engine wiring harness would have to be taken out and either repaired or replaced. Mike One-Three was now sitting inside a huge hangar and the guys who were working on it gave us cots to sleep on so we wouldn't have to sleep on the cement floor. They even showed us where the hot showers and mess hall were located. This wasn't going to be so bad after all. My guys thought it was going to be a real vacation until I informed them that we could do some of our own maintenance. So for the next three days, we replaced the worn-out road wheels and support rollers and were even able to replace a small section of track.

At night after our showers (we were getting spoiled by that hot water), we walked up the hill to the small NCO Club. I'll never forget, they made the best Tom Collins I've ever had. I can taste them right now as I write this. They were tall, cold, and handmade with fresh, squeezed lemons and all. This nice little club even had a band on the weekends. I had almost forgot what a weekend was. We didn't do those in our tank company. My guys sure had a good time.

Despite the comfy surroundings, I was getting bored by the sixth day and really wanted to get back to our unit. Even the floorshow at the club couldn't keep me from wanting to leave. I walked into the hangar unexpected on that sixth day and caught the sergeant off-guard. I found the maintenance people pulling out the new harness!

"What are you guys doing?! Is something wrong?" I questioned.

"We finished the job yesterday, but we're so bored we were going to do it again," he confessed.

"You've got to be kidding, right?" I asked but he said no and if we didn't tell anyone, he'd have us on the road by late the next night. I agreed and headed to the club for a Tom Collins.

At dawn on the eighth day, Mike One-Three was on the road and heading for Xuan Loc. Picking up speed on the main road, I yelled, "Kick it in the ass, Harry. Let's get our butts home!" Black smoke bellowed out of the back of the tank as it lunged forward and rumbled out of sight. Watch out for that car, Harry! Just another day in the 'Nam.

The Day the Music Stopped

We had driven all night to get here and the men of the first and second platoons of M company were exhausted. A platoon of ACAVs - the armored cavalry assault vehicles also known as tracks - from K troop had been overrun seven hours earlier in the darkness of the night. By the time we arrived, you wouldn't have known anything had ever happened. The still operable K troop tracks had left the battle scene and the two damaged and burned ones had already been hauled away. The only reminder of any kind of fight was the large section of charred ground where one of the tracks had caught fire and burned. The three remaining platoons from K troop along with the tracks of I troop were now busy combing a five-mile search area around the scene looking for the Viet Cong soldiers who had successfully attacked our men the night before.

Our ten tanks started the task of setting up a perimeter with the medic and communications tracks and the company commander's (CO) tank in the middle. I told Harry, my driver, to pull up a little until we were aligned with the tanks on either side of us. Then I hollered to Chopper, my gunner, to take the guard position so I could get a closer look at our new surroundings.

The terrain was pretty flat and the areas behind and to the far sides were nothing but thick, green vegetation and triple canopy jungle. However, the area to the front of my tank was a completely different matter. It was wide open to the rolling hills 200 yards away, except for a few four-foot high, four-foot thick hedgerows of brush that were scattered about. Although this spot was far from ideal, with so many tanks in one place it was the best we could find and it would have to do for now. We would wait until the enemy was found and the fierce firepower of our 90mm cannons was needed.

I walked back to the front of our tank and told Harry to shut it down and for him and Strickland to check the suspension. Then I called to Chopper to take the guard since I was going over to talk with the platoon sergeant. As I walked away, I became concerned

33

with the wide-open space directly to our front and wanted to make sure there was plenty of barbed wire put out tonight. Our CO was also obviously concerned about our location because he told the two platoon sergeants to set up additional two-man guard posts around the outside of the perimeter.

We spent the rest of the day pulling maintenance, getting our tanks topped off with fuel, and trying to get a little rest. I took the guard position on top of the commander's hatch while my crew got washed. I saw that two members of our platoon had been positioned about fifty yards to the front of my tank and just inside of one of those thick, wide bushes. That shrub was so dense that I couldn't understand what possible good these soldiers were going to do because they couldn't have been able to see through it. They should have been positioned on the other side so they could've seen any approaching enemy.

It was about then that I realized it was time for my favorite radio program. Whenever possible, we tried to listen to the rock and roll show that came on at 3:00 P.M. on Armed Forces Radio. I located my transistor radio in the turret and Harry climbed down into his driver's compartment to enjoy the familiar back-home sounds.

The disc jockey was playing "Little Surfer Girl" by the Beach Boys, one of my favorites. I was singing along with them while casually scanning the area to our front, more out of habit than anything. I started with the tank to my left, scanned the two clumps of brush, then over to the next larger bush where our two guys were positioned, over to the strip of jungle, and finally back to the tank on my right. I was really getting down with the music as I continued my visual sweep of the area. First the tank on the left, then the two small bushes, then the four men by the large bush. *Four men? Did I say four men? There should only be two!* About that same time I heard the loud familiar POP! of a rocket. Then I saw it. The small black dot grew larger and larger is as got closer. It was a Communist rocket-propelled grenade (RPG) and it was headed straight at us. I sat there hypnotized in disbelief. Seconds later, I heard the whoosh as it flew past me only inches above my head. It cut the tank radio antenna in half before exploding to my rear in the center of the perimeter. "Incoming!" I yelled as loud as I could while pulling back the charging handle of my 50-caliber machine gun. Normally, I would have fired a main gun round but I couldn't because of the two Cavalry troopers behind that bush. They were now lying face down on the ground with their hands over their heads right between me and the VC. The enemy had been on the other side of that same bush when they fired the RPG and it naturally scared the hell out of those guys. It went directly over their heads and both of them hit the dirt not knowing what to do next. After all, they weren't infantry men, just scared tankers. They then stood up, scrambling toward the relative safety of our perimeter, but they were still right in my line of fire!

I hollered over the tank radio telling everyone the enemy was to our front and that I still couldn't fire because two of our men were in the way. Instead, I fired the 50-caliber over their heads and watched helplessly as the VC reloaded their rocket launcher. POP! a second round fired off and headed right at my tank. I heard Harry crank up the tank to supply the needed electrical power for the turret. Seconds later I realized that second slow-flying RPG was going to hit our tank. I jumped off the side of the turret just as the round exploded below the 50-caliber machine gun. Chunks of hot steel flew everywhere and my transistor radio disappeared into a thousand tiny pieces.

I felt the heat of the explosion and small pieces of metal and plastic dug deep into my face and chest. The last thing I remember thinking was *There go my sounds!* The force of the explosion blew me high above the tank and then I started falling back down to the ground some twenty feet below. Instead of hitting the ground, I found myself falling into a deep, dark, black hole. I was scared and tried to get my balance when I saw a bright and glowing light. In a matter of seconds, I drifted into the middle of a long tunnel filled with constantly changing colored lights. Visions of every joyous occasion from my past suddenly flashed before my eyes. It's difficult to put into words the sights and feelings I experienced because they can't be compared to anything in reality.

I became completely engulfed by an overpowering feeling of inner warmth and contentment all at the same time. I was no longer worried or afraid as I slid through this wonderfully welcoming light which enveloped me. Ever so slowly, I landed on my feet in a breathtaking green meadow where bright yellow daisies covered the rolling hills and the blue sky seemed to go on forever. Could this be Fiddlers' Green, the place where all cavalry troopers go to rest?

Then I experienced a feeling of love ten times greater than the warmth of any human love I'd ever known on earth. It seemed to explode from deep within my being. I felt neither pain nor fear as I walked toward a small group of people dressed in white who were approaching me with open arms. Nobody spoke. Nobody had to. I could understand everything they were thinking. An enormous rainbow appeared across the sky. Somehow I seemed to know these people as friends and relatives from my past. Although some of them had died long before I was ever born, it was like I had always known them. We stood together and mentally communicated for what seemed like a very long time. Love surrounded us and an overwhelming feeling of complete happiness filled the air.

We walked down a winding, narrow dirt road that disappeared into a large white cloud. About halfway down the road, I saw my mother and father, who had died a few years before, standing next to a wooden fence that ran alongside the path. My mom looked very young and wore a single daisy in her hair. My dad also looked quite young, around twenty-five years old. He was wearing his Army dress uniform with his shiny second lieutenant bars glittering in the sunlight. *Perhaps this was when they had been their happiest,* I thought. They waved at me and I smiled and waved back. When they then joined the group, we hugged and my sense of contentment grew even stronger.

As we reached the end of the road, the white cloud slowly parted and a pair of large wooden doors opened. As I walked alone toward them, a very bright, clear light encircled me. Then a resonant, yet reassuring voice spoke to me.

"Jack, are you ready to come with me?"

I remember this quite clearly. I replied, "Hell no, I can't go with you. I'm only twenty-two!

Even as I blurted out those words, I knew that going back would be one of the hardest decisions I would ever have to make. It was so wonderful and peaceful here.

As soon as those words escaped my lips, I found myself lying on the ground next to my tank. I shook my head to get my bearings and with blood-covered hands, climbed up the side of the tank to the commander's hatch. Once there, I saw that the two troopers had gotten out of my field of fire and were running like crazy past my left side. I reconnected the communications cord to my helmet and quickly fired a main gun round. It hit short of the bush.

Strickland, who was now inside of the turret reloading the main gun, yelled, "Up!" I tried to set my sights on the two VC soldiers who were running away, but everything was a blur. Blood was running down my face and affected my vision. I heard another tank fire. At that same time, a call came from the CO's tank. He screamed, "Mike One-Three, I told you to fire, you damn coward! Now fire!"

Without even thinking, I slammed the turret hard to the right and rotated my gun tube the full 180 degrees, knocking my loader to the turret floor in the process.

My gun tube was now facing directly at the CO's tank and as I reached for the main gun trigger, I screamed back, "I'll show you a coward, you sonofabitch!" I was wiping blood from eyes and Strickland was yelling at me to stop. I must have been in shock.

Our platoon leader arrived out of nowhere, grabbed me by my shoulders, and yanked me out of the hatch. "What the hell is going on over here?!" he demanded. But before I could explain, he noticed my wounds and called for a medic. I continued demanding an apology from the CO as they carried me to the medic track.

By the time I reached the medic track, the two enemy soldiers were dead, but not before firing at least six rockets into our perimeter. A gunship support had been called in and they picked off the VC in the open field less than 800 yards from our perimeter.

I lost two front teeth and had wounds on my head and shoulders, but had somehow survived this terrible day. Later, I would receive my first Purple Heart for those wounds, but I never got what I really wanted - an apology.

It took almost thirty years to realize the full significance of my near-death experience. On the afternoon of 6 September 1997, I was standing behind the podium in the hospital chapel at Fort Campbell, Kentucky, at a memorial service for my second oldest son, Jon K. Stoddard, who had died a week earlier.

It had been a long, emotional drive from my home in Las Vegas, Nevada, and I was both mentally and physically drained as I sat in the Chaplain's small office the day before the service. My oldest son, Jack III, and his mother, my ex-wife Ginny, were also there. Both of them were showing signs of shock over Jon's untimely death and Ginny, who had raised both boys while I was in Vietnam, was a nervous wreck despite strong medication.

The base Chaplain asked me who was going offer the eulogy for Jon. He could readily see that his mother was in no condition to do it and so I suggested that perhaps Jack Jr. would be appropriate. However, when a panicked look shot across his face and tears trickled down his cheeks, I knew that was out of the question. That left me. I told the Chaplain I would do it even though, at the time, I had no idea what I could say. We left the small basement office and I returned to my motel room alone with my thoughts.

I had to get some much needed sleep. Although exhausted, it would not come easily. I spent much of that night tossing and turning thinking about what I would say the next day.

Everything seemed surreal as I took my place behind the podium. As I started to speak, I looked into the grieving faces of Ginny, her mother, her two sisters, and my oldest son, Jack. I felt all those eyes on me. I began.

"All of us who knew Jon will retain our own special memories of him that we will carry with us forever and that, perhaps, is the way he should be best remembered. Mine is to remember him as a young boy playing in his very first baseball game. Jon had his ups and downs in his short life and was by no means perfect. He was just like any other young man his age and I loved him with all my heart. Rather than stand here and tell you how great he was, I would like to tell you where I believe he is now and how he's doing."

I could see the puzzled looks on everyone's faces as I continued. I knew I couldn't keep going without crying myself, so I asked them all to close their eyes and take a journey with me. I explained that I had taken this same trip more than three decades ago, the year before Jon was born, when I was a young soldier in a faraway placed called Vietnam. I then proceeded to tell them about my near-death experience. I took them to heaven's gate and told them about that hallowed place called Fiddlers' Green and the peaceful, happy place that Jon now called home. I closed my speech with, "Jon, we miss you and love you."

I hoped my little story helped everyone, especially Ginny and Jack, in their time of greatest need. Giving that eulogy had been among the hardest things I ever had to do. I hope I did it right, Jon. I really wanted to.

Give Me Hope

Those infantry soldiers really thought us tankers had it made. The grunts had to carry everything they owned with them. They had to walk across Vietnam wearing seventy-pound packs and had to sleep on the ground with only a poncho to keep them warm on cold and rainy nights. Day in and day out, they ambled though the mud, swamps, and rice paddies while the tankers of M company just drove around them. They really envied us. As far as they were concerned, we might as well have been in a Winnebago. I must admit, we did have a few more comforts, but we were also a much bigger target.

There wasn't a soft spot on the whole tank. I had to put my flack jacket on top of the commander's hatch to give my butt something soft to sit on. But mile after mile of bouncing around eventually took its toll on me. For more than a week now my butt had really been hurting and finally Harry, my driver on Mike One-Three, came up to me one day and said, "Sarge, you have to go see Doc and get your sore butt looked at. We're getting tired of being yelled at because you're in such a bad mood!"

"Okay. Yeah, I know I've been in a foul mood lately. I'll go over and have him check it out."

"Why don't you go over now? I saw two of our medics standing by their track a minute ago." Harry said.

"Okay, I'll go. Just watch me!" He knew I hated going to see the Doc almost as much as I hated the enemy!

As I carefully climbed my way off of the tank I was in pain, but I didn't want my guys to know it. I yelled up to Harry to throw me down my helmet. After catching it, I sauntered over to the two medics in the middle of our perimeter. I heard Harry and Chopper laughing in the background.

Approaching the medic track, I saw Doc Brown and Doc Edwards both standing at the rear. The ramp was lowered to the ground and they had built a small cooking area and had some cans of C rations warming over a heat tablet. It must have been lunch time. When I got close to them I called out, "What's for lunch, guys?"

"Beanie weenies," they chimed. "You want some, Jack?"

"No, no, that's all I need with my sore butt," I answered back.

"Sore butt huh? Well, sit down over there and we'll take a look in a minute."

Soon their lunch was over and Doc Brown reached into his bag and pulled out a pair of rubber gloves. Doc Brown was the oldest of the two medics, being at least twenty. He finally said, "Okay, Jack, drop your pants and grab your boots." I was a little embarrassed but they added, "We've seen more butts than you can shake a stick at!" I did what was requested of me.

So here I was in the middle of the perimeter, pants down and bent over holding on to my legs while two guys are checking out my ass. That is humiliating in every sense of the word!

"Yep," the medics said as they took turns checking me out.

"Just what I thought," one said to the other. You got hemorrhoids, and they're pretty bad, too," was the finally verdict.

Being a naïve, twenty-two-year-old, I had no idea what these guys were talking about. I asked, "What's that? What's a hemorrhoid anyway?"

Well, you would have thought I'd just told them the funniest joke in the world because they both dropped to the ground laughing and yelled out, "It's no big thing, Jack. It's just when all your guts fall out through your ass and land on the ground!"

They must have seen the look in my eyes as I stammered out, "What? My guts are falling out of my ass?!"

"No, it's not really that bad," laughed Doc Brown as he and Doc Edwards were trying to get themselves up off the ground.

After everything was settled down, it was decided I'd have to take the evening chow chopper back to base camp and get my hemorrhoids inspected at the base hospital. Doc Brown gave me one of those red medical tags to take with me and I headed back to my tank to let my guys know what was going on. I also stopped by the platoon sergeant's tank to let him know. It didn't take long after that before every man in the perimeter knew that Sgt. Stoddard had hemorrhoids!

The chopper ride was a little rough on my sore butt. Thank goodness it wasn't a very long trip. The pilots landed just outside the hospital and it wasn't long before I reported in. I was then taken to a small room where a nurse told me to drop my drawers once again. She told me to report back to them at five the next morning and to bring my shaving kit with me. I was going to fly out to the USS Hope, a large hospital ship located three miles off shore in the South China Sea, to get my hemorrhoids taken care of. As quick as I could, I got back to the orderly room to let them know what was going on. I slept real good that night, dreaming of just lying around on the cruise ship drinking iced tea and recuperating. This was going to be the life.

At first light, I was standing in front of the hospital in a brand new uniform with shined boots holding my tattered and worn shaving kit. I was ready to start my vacation! There were four of us that took the medical chopper to Cam Ranh Bay where we transferred to another chopper for the thirty-minute flight out to the ship. It was really cool flying over the ocean watching the fish swimming in the crystal clear blue water below. Before long, we saw the USS Hope below. Boy, was it huge! The landing was a little rough because the ship was pitching and rolling, but we managed to unload okay and were directed by a sailor in bell-bottom blue jeans to enter through a large metal hatch (I think that's what they call their doors). The four of us were then taken to a small cabin where our red tags were looked at and we were directed where to go.

It took me more than an hour to find the cabin where I was to report. On the way, though, I did manage to locate two snack bars, one movie theater, and a place called the Captain's Store where candy and stuff like that was sold. This place was great. I knew I'd be having a good time on this ship. I finally walked inside the cabin marked 336C and reported to two very young looking sailors in green scrubs.

43

"Hi, guys, I was told to report here." I handed them my stack of papers that were now smeared with chocolate.

After looking at my records, they told me to get undressed and put on the paper robe they handed me. No problem, I could handle that and I was soon standing there with a cold breeze on my backside. Next, they asked me to sit in this large leather chair. That wasn't too bad either, maybe just a little cold was all. I was thinking how easy this was when I was told to hold on and they suddenly flipped the damn chair upside down. My bare ass was now sticking straight up in the air! I knew things were only going to get worse when they approached me, one with a giant needle in his hands.

I was told this operation (I wasn't planning on an operation!) would only take a few minutes, but they would have to give me four shots around the infected area. I don't know what they were thinking, but to me it sounded like they wanted to shoot me in my asshole! That didn't sound very cool to me, but what came next was anything but cool.

When they gave me the first shot, I screamed out, "Holy shit! I've been shot and it didn't hurt like this!" I was breaking out in a cold sweat. "You guys have got to cut me some slack. You're killing me here!"

They just smiled and said, "After the next one, you won't feel a thing."

They were right. I think I had gone into shock by then.

Thirty minutes later, I was once again standing on the deck and feeling no pain. I was numb from the waist down. These two doctors (at least I hoped they were doctors!) told me to relax for a little while and then report back to the main desk where I had checked in two hours earlier. Before long, I was waddling down the ship's halls with a Kotex between my legs. A vacation this wasn't!

The return flight seemed twice as long as I sat on my new rubber donut and stared out the chopper window. It was dark when I finally reached my base camp at Xuan Loc. I waddled the half-mile back to the orderly room and reported in.

The first sergeant looked over my papers and said, "Good, we need another guy to work CQ here at night. See you tomorrow for duty, Sergeant" I then returned to my hooch and soaked my butt.

At 6:00 A.M. the next day, I was on my way to the motor pool looking for a ride back out to my platoon. I wasn't here to work in an office. I was a combat soldier, sore butt and all! In less than thirty minutes, I was heading out the main gate on the way back to my platoon.

The Redheaded Lieutenant

It was another one of those typically hot, sticky Vietnam days. I was sitting on the tank commander's seat drinking a warm Coke and watching our newly assigned platoon leader walk around our small group of tanks as he got acquainted with his new troops. Today was his first day, having arrived by jeep to our location only a few hours earlier. Our former platoon leader, First Lieutenant Jacobs, had been reassigned to a staff job for the last six months of his tour.

For the past four days, this very young new second lieutenant named Todd was busy in-processing and becoming familiar with his new command. While we both appeared to be about the same age, the big difference between us was I'd already been in the 'Nam for nine months.

Lieutenant Todd was busy talking to the crew from Mike One-Two. As I watched him, I was thinking how it must feel to be a twenty-two-year-old platoon leader. That had to be a heavy load for any young soldier to carry. It was hard enough taking care of one tank, let alone being responsible for five of them. I sure hoped Sergeant First Class Edwards would take Lt. Todd under his wing. It was the old soldiers like Edwards who kept us younger ones alive.

He finally arrived at my tank, Hang 'Em High (after the Clint Eastwood movie). He talked to Chopper and Strickland who were nervously hemming and hawing around trying to answer his questions. The young lieutenant then climbed up on the tank and held his hand out, "You must be Sgt. Stoddard. I'm Lt. Todd."

"Yes, sir," I said. "Welcome to the platoon." Boy did he look young! Even younger than me. He was a little taller, with freckle-covered fair skin and the reddest hair I'd ever seen.

"Are you guys authorized to hang that skull from the end of your gun tube?" he questioned.

"Well, nobody's told us to take it down, sir." I answered.

"Oh, okay. How long have you been in the platoon, Sergeant?

"About nine months, sir." I replied trying to hide my unpolished, almost white suede looking boots.

"Sure is a hot one today, isn't it?"

"Yes, sir, it's plenty hot now, but by the time we get our logger and NDP set up tonight, it'll be a lot cooler."

"What's a logger?" Lt. Todd inquired.

I hoped that he was only kidding, but I went ahead and explained it to him anyway. "Sir, that's when we back all our tanks into a very tight circle with the front ends and gun tubes facing outward. We do this mostly at night. It's sort of like what the wagon trains did in the Old West to protect themselves from the Indians. Only we don't have to worry about bows and arrows out here ,sir, just the VC and their RPGs!"

I was laughing at my own joke when he asked, "Well then, what's an NDP?"

I was beginning to get a little worried about this guy. Didn't they teach them anything at officer school? Giving him the benefit of the doubt, I thought maybe he was just testing me. In any event, I continued, "Well, sir, a Night Defensive Perimeter, or NDP for short, is when the five tanks in a platoon form a circle. Then all of the crews, with the exception of the man on guard duty, lay out the barbed wire that is carried on the rear of each tank. Next, the crews position trip flares outside the wire at intervals of every ten to twenty feet and hidden from view as best as possible. Then come the claymores. Each tank crew puts out four of these mines and aligns them so when they explode, the spray of pellets will be staggered. Each tank is then responsible for its own field of fire, or view, which includes the visible areas of the two tanks on either side of them. That way no portion of the perimeter goes unchecked. Well, that pretty well sums it up, sir."

The young lieutenant smiled approvingly. "That was great, Sgt. Stoddard. You really know your stuff."

I just smiled thinking to myself, *Betcha I was driving a tank before you even knew what one looked like.* Better judgement told me to keep my mouth shut for a change and I just said simply,

"Thank you, sir." In any event, apparently I'd passed his test, if that's what it was.

For the past five days, our platoon had been providing road and convoy security about thirty miles outside of Xuan Loc on Highway One which was the main artery through South Vietnam and stretching all the way to the North Vietnam border. As it was literally our lifeline to the rest of the world, it was critical to keep it clear of mines and enemy ambushes. Security for this particular stretch of the road between Saigon and Xuan Loc where our base camp was located was assigned to our regiment. Everyday, convoys were on the road, three of them in the morning and three of them in the afternoon, with the last one being off the road by 6:00 P.M. After that time, the road belonged to only us. If anything moved, we assumed it was Charlie and was fair game.

The first couple of days of our detail were usually consumed with pulling routine tank maintenance. By the third day, we were cleaning personal gear and writing letters home and on the fourth day, boredom set in so the cards came out for an afternoon game. Don't get me wrong. We all knew this job and although it was monotonous at times, it was nevertheless an important one. It's just that there wasn't much action in the way of enemy contact.

Later that evening while we were setting up our NDP, a supply chopper landed outside the perimeter. It was loaded with hot chow and mail, two of the things we looked forward to the most in the 'Nam. It took another hour before we were finished with our work and my guys could finally get some hot chow. Strickland brought me back a plate of fried chicken, my very favorite, and also handed me two letters from home. From the scent, I knew they were from my wife, Ginny. I tucked them inside my shirt pocket to read later in private.

It was getting dark, so we settled in for the night. At 2:50 A.M., Harry got me up for guard duty. I always pulled the same watch because I wanted to make sure nobody had fallen asleep. My crew knew I took this guard stuff seriously and that I'd punish anybody who messed up.

49

I took my position in the tank commander's hatch behind my 50-caliber machine gun and turned on my new transistor radio. With the volume set low, I listened to music from home. When my eyes adjusted to the blackness around me, I scanned our field of fire trying to recognize some of the same objects I had seen earlier in the daylight. At night, the jungle took on an entirely different appearance.

I both loved and hated this time of the morning. I loved it because it was during these quiet hours that I could sip my hot chocolate and think of home and watch the sun rise up over the beautiful but dangerous, jungle. I hated it because this was when we were the most vulnerable to attack. As the night struggled into day, our exposed tanks would be silhouetted against the ever brightening sky, becoming perfect targets, yet we couldn't see into the still black jungle. This is when the VC would usually attack their prey. But on this night, the first platoon of M company would again be victorious. We had made it safely through another night and were ready to start a new day.

By 6:00 A.M., we had torn down our NDP site. I knew this was going to be a great day because I'd found a can of eggs with ham chunks for breakfast! We moved our tanks two miles down the highway and into a large open field that was mostly covered with four-foot tall elephant grass. This is where we would spend the last day of road security. It was real quiet in the morning and by 11:00 A.M., we were ready to start our first game of poker. Four of us tank commanders sat on the back deck of Mike One-Four figuring out which game to play and hoping to get the new lieutenant into it. After all, he must have had some money on him with just arriving in country and all.

The four of us schemed to work together to relieve him of his money and then we'd split it up later. Boy, did we plan this one right. In less than a half-hour, the lieutenant was climbing up the side of the tank.

"Hi, Lieutenant. How are you doing this morning, sir?" we all said in unison.

"You guys mind if I sit in for a while?"

50

He said just what we hoped he would. "No, not at all, sir. We're not very good, but we have fun."

Nothing else was happening as far as our support mission anyway and by 2:00 P.M., we were the proud possessors of almost a hundred dollars of the LT's money. We decided to give him a break and call off this slaughter. Besides, a small band of local camp followers had arrived at our location.

It seemed to always be the same group who showed up whenever tankers were working along the main highway: two small boys selling Cokes and beer, another kid selling chunks of melting ice wrapped in straw and an old burlap bag, two young and generally not so good-looking hookers ("boom-boom" girls the GIs called them) and their old mamasan who was in charge of negotiations. Sometimes she would also wash your clothes for you for a separate sum if there was a stream nearby.

We went to check out the girls and get a Coke, leaving the lieutenant standing on the back deck of the tank. An hour or so later, I was standing behind our tank talking with Chopper when the LT walked up to us.

"Can I talk to you for a minute, Sergeant?" he asked me.

"Sure, sir, what can I do for you?" I said as we walked away from the tank.

"Are those girls any good?" He was pointing at the boom-boom girls who were flirting with a couple of GIs.

"Well," I said, "they're not as good as the ones in Saigon, but they're okay I guess, why?"

"I was thinking maybe I'd..." I cut him off in mid-sentence and told him to go over in the elephant grass in the middle of the perimeter and that I'd send the prettiest girl over to him. I also told him to make sure he didn't pay any more than ten dollars.

After telling the girl where to go, I naturally had to let everyone else know what was about to take place. I made the rounds of all the tanks and the crews all climbed up on their turrets to get a good look. When I told our platoon sergeant, SFC Edwards, he just shook his head and said, "You're a crazy SOB, Jack." All the tankers now had a great view of Lt. Todd and the hooker bouncing

51

up and down in the grass. In no time, we were all cracking up at the site of the whitest butt any of us had ever seen!

What happened next to our young lieutenant was something that even I could not have anticipated. We all heard the familiar POP POP POP POP of rotor blades and looked up to see one of our helicopters bringing out our company commander. He was here for a surprise inspection. Surprise was right! You should have seen that poor lieutenant jump up, pull his pants on, and run all at the same time. His face was as red as his hair. He shot off in one direction and the boom-boom girl took off in the other. Nobody could have planned it more perfectly! It sure was something to behold. Of course, poor Lt. Todd got his butt chewed royally, no pun intended, but none of us were bored the rest of the day that was for sure. Our naive young lieutenant had grown up real fast. Welcome to the first platoon, LT. Your life will never be the same.

*the story is true, but Lt. Todd is a fictitious name

Row, Row, Row Your Boat

The monsoon season was here and the last few days had been really miserable. The first platoon of M company had once again been assigned the boring but important task of road security. So far, nothing spectacular had happened along our assigned sector.

Around 1:00 P.M., our platoon sergeant, Sergeant First Class Edwards, stood up on the back deck of his tank, waved his arms in a circular motion, and yelled, "Tank commanders on me!"

In tanker talk, that meant for us commanders to get our asses over there in a hurry! I grabbed my helmet. As I was getting off my tank, I told my loader to take the watch. Wiping the rain from my eyes, I ran over to the rear of SFC Edwards' tank.

It only took a few minutes until all four of us tank commanders were huddled under the huge tarp that was hung from the side of his tank. *At least we were* dry, I thought reaching for my pack of smokes. After all faces were wiped dry, cigarettes lit, and the normal horseplay was at a minimum, SFC Edwards said, "Listen up, you wise guys. I just got word we're going on a river patrol mission with the ARVNs tonight, so get your tanks ready to pull out of here in one hour. And I mean tie everything down good! I don't want to lose anything on this trip!" One of the guys had lost his duffel bag while we were on our way here and that really pissed off the sergeant.

I was excited as I walked back to my tank, as this was the first time I'd ever worked with any ARVN (Army of the Republic of South Vietnam) soldiers and also the first time to pull a river patrol, whatever that was. I climbed back on my tank and yelled for everyone to get ready to move out within the hour and make sure everything was secured. We were soon pulling out onto Highway One, the tank tracks hurling giant clumps of mud onto its clean surface.

The rain had stopped for now and the trip toward Ben Hoa was a pleasant one. Just before we got there we turned off the main highway and started down a muddy side road which would take us

53

to our predetermined night defensive perimeter, a small grassy knoll about twenty feet above and overlooking the river.

Ten minutes after we turned onto the side road, we came to a small hamlet consisting of four bamboo huts, two on each side of the road. There was a large black kettle with white steam coming out of it sitting on top of a roaring fire in front of two of the huts. Pigs were scurrying everywhere and I had to yell at Harry, my driver, to slow down and be careful of them. It was a tight squeeze, but soon all of our tanks made it through leaving everything unscathed.

It only took another ten minutes before we found ourselves facing a large rice paddy. We slowly maneuvered our tanks around the outer edges until we found the small grassy knoll one hundred yards away. It took us a half-hour there because we had to move so slowly. One false move and you could bury your tank in the quicksand-like mud.

We finally made it and SFC Edwards pointed at me to put my tank in the most forward position facing the river. I could see the brown water extending straight out in front of me for 300 yards until it slowly banked off to the left and disappeared. It reminded me of the Russian River back home in Guerneville, California.

I had to ground guide Chopper into position because the dirt was soft and I didn't want my fifty-ton tank dropping into the muddy brown water below us. Mike One-Two took the position to my left while the other three tanks took up their positions facing toward the rice paddy and small hamlet behind it.

In twenty minutes, we pretty much had our perimeter set up except for the barbed wire and flares. Those would come later when it got a little darker. We had been informed a platoon-sized unit of ARVN Rangers would be here around 4:00 P.M. and for us to be nice to them and support them the best we could.

Sure enough, a bit later we could see the twenty-eight Rangers walking toward our location. They even had two girls on a moped with them! It turned out these women were the wives of two of the soldiers and they were here to cook their nightly dinners. Like I said, this was the first time I'd ever worked around these soldiers and I thought how tidy they all looked in their skintight, tailored uniforms. The second thing I noticed was they didn't seem to be carrying a lot of ammunition. Maybe the girls would go back and get it on their moped.

To most of us in Vietnam, the ARVNs were considered a strange bunch. It seemed to me that they didn't take the war as seriously as we did. But then again, we were only here for a year and they were here forever. Their war started even before some of them were born. It's all they knew. A lot of times, the ARVN's entire family would go into battle acting as nurses, cooks, and even doing the laundry while the men were out on patrol. No matter what you thought of our brother soldiers, you had to respect them for fighting for their own freedom.

As we all sat around eating our C's (rations), you could smell the fish and rice our brother soldiers were eating. I don't know why, but those C-rations tasted extra good that evening! Soon it was getting dark and as the last of our trip flares were in position, I was wishing the rangers would settle down a little. They were all busy cleaning their pots and pans below my position on the riverbank. I think one of them was actually taking a bath, too!

We had talked with Lieutenant Elway, the ARVNs American advisor, who told us a lot of enemy traffic had been moving down this river the past few days. I found this sort of exciting, but still didn't really understand what good a tank sitting up on a riverbank was going to do. I figured the ARVNs could handle this by themselves.

After making sure everything was set for the night, I doubled-checked all the weapons and assigned the guard order for the night. I'd be pulling my usual watch from three to six in the morning. Once that was done, we settled in for the night. Lt. Elway asked if he could sleep on my back deck and I said, "Sure, LT, what ever turns your crank." My guys had laid their sleeping bags behind our tank and I would sleep inside the turret as I always did.

Strickland, my loader, woke me up at ten minutes to three. I hadn't gotten much sleep during the night between the mosquitoes biting me and all the ARVNs talking around the perimeter. It was a wonder every Viet Cong within a hundred-mile radius didn't know we were here! But soon I was getting settled into my routine of lighting my one-man stove to make my cocoa and taking a good look around my field of fire. After I got my eyes adjusted to the dark, I could see pretty good since the full moon was casting its yellow glow upon the water. Every once in a while, I would get hit with a drop of rain and I knew it would only be a matter of time until the morning monsoon rains would be coming across our position in the form of a solid sheets.

As I was putting on my rain jacket, I heard this splashing sound off in the direction of the river. My first thought was, *I can't believe those ARVNs are taking a bath!* But then I heard the splashing sound again and this time it was getting closer! I leaned around the tank commander's hatch and whispered to Lt. Elway, "Sir, I think I hear something in the river."

I heard it again. Splash, splash, splash. Suddenly, I realized it was someone paddling a boat down the river. Not waiting for a response from the LT, I dropped down to the gunner's seat to get a better look through the main gun telescope. Looking through the scope, I rotated the gun to the left using the manual hand cranks and found my target, two VC rowing a wooden canoe right at us. They were less than fifty yards up river. I assumed they were VC because the river was a free-fire zone at night and all the locals knew the water ways were off-limits. Since the 30-caliber machine gun switch was always in the fire position at night, all I had to do was pull the trigger.

I looked up at the tank commander's hatch opening and in accordance with procedure, yelled to the lieutenant first in a soft voice, "Machine gun." And then a little louder, "On the way!" I refocused and put the crosshairs just in front of the canoe. I pulled the trigger and immediately saw the red tracer bullets crossing the water and blowing pieces of wood off the bow of the boat. I walked the bullets a little higher until I could see the first man in the boat. Because of the magnification of the telescope, he looked so close that it was like he was right in front of me. The closeness kind of intimidated me a bit. I'd never had to fire on anyone at such close range before.

I turned the gun upward and put about a half dozen rounds through his body before he fell into the water. As he fell, the oar in his hand came into sight and it surprised me how fast the rounds cut it in half. I thought, *Holy shit!*

Up until then, my adrenaline had been controlling my actions, but now I started to remember my surroundings and was a little concerned about our ARVN friends. I hoped none of them were in front of the main gun. My next thought was, *Oh well, too late if they are.*

I continued to work my machine gun fire until I was at the far end of the boat. I was starting to worry about it moving out of my target range so I decided to fire a main gun round. Once again I yelled, only louder this time, "Main gun, on the way!" I laid my crosshairs on the man in the rear of the canoe and pulled the trigger. There was a loud BANG as the 90mm breech recoiled and the tank rocked backward. Instantaneously, I saw wood chunks flying everywhere and the man who I'd seen in the scope was now completely gone from sight. My only thought was, *Jack, I think you overdid it a bit with that canister round.* The canoe that had been only thirty feet from me at the time was now only pieces of wood floating downstream.

Once again, it was quiet and I found myself shaking slightly as I climbed out of the hot turret and into the fresh air. While all that was going on (about three minutes), the ARVN platoon sergeant had climbed onto the back deck when the machine gun fire started. He was excited, jumping and up and down telling the American lieutenant, "VC, VC, they get away!" At that same time, the main gun went off and he looked at the lieutenant and said, "No VC. They no get away." We all had a good laugh about that one.

As we were talking, this ARVN Ranger came running in front of my tank yelling and screaming and holding his head with both hands. The guy reminded me of a chicken with its head cut off. Finally, three guys tackled and held him to the ground as our medic ran over to help. It turned out the ranger had put his hammock up on the side of my tank using the end connectors to keep it in place. Well, as I rotated the gun tube to follow my target, it had moved directly over his sleeping position and when I fired the canister round, the concussion blew his eardrums out. I felt bad for my brother soldier, but I just didn't realize he was under the gun tube. He really had no business being there.

Remembering my cup of cocoa, I went back in the turret to get it. I heard the medevac chopper landing to take this poor soul to the hospital.

Many months later when I was out-processing from the regiment, I had to clear the awards and decorations section. I figured I'd ask if I had been put in for any kind of award for my actions that morning. One of the clerks said my story did sound familiar so he checked into it. A few minutes later, he handed me a copy of orders for a Silver Star that was awarded to Lt. Elway.

I stood there dumbfounded for a few seconds and finally said, "I can't believe this shit, but what are you gonna do?" The clerks told me they thought I should have gotten the award, too. Walking out the door, one of them yelled, "I'd go kick his ass, Sarge. What are they going to do, send you to Vietnam?"

Section Two

My New Unit-Air Rifle Platoon, Air Cavalry Troop, 11th Armored Cavalry Regiment

♦ Wearing of the Black Beret

♦ ARPs, My First Mission

♦ Back to Michelin

♦ Another Day in the ARPs

♦ Night Ambush

♦ A Surprise for Charlie

♦ Just One of Those Days

Wearing of the Black Beret

The 11th Armored Cavalry Regiment has two mottos. The first one, "Allons," was given to the regiment in the early 1900s. The second one, "Find The Bastards, Then Pile On," was given while in Vietnam. It is the unofficial motto, but the one I think tells it all. Some say this motto was given by the then current regimental commander, Colonel George S. Patton III, but others say it was given by General Depuy who was the First Cavalry Division commander. It doesn't really matter who gave us the motto as they couldn't have picked a more precise one.

The 11th Armored Cavalry Regiment was one of the most feared combat units in Vietnam. I don't think there was a VC or NVA (North Vietnamese Army) soldier who didn't fear and hate the enemy who wore the Blackhorse patch on their shoulder. I'm not saying that just because I served with the unit (I served in other units as well), but because it was the truth.

First into battle was the ARPs (Aero Rifle Platoon) of the Air Cavalry Troop. It was their job to locate the enemy. After they located them, next would come rest of the Blackhorse troop - the tank companies, ACAVs (armored cavalry assault vehicles) filled with troops, and finally the artillery batteries. The regiment would pile on the enemy and literally force them back into their holes deep within the jungle floor.

Besides being first in, the other mission was to protect and to rescue their downed pilots. Being a member of the ARPs was a very demanding job. There were good missions and bad missions and sometimes they never wanted to go back out again, but they did because they loved and respected their fellow ARPs more than life itself.

It was monsoon season in late 1968 when I first saw a soldier wearing a black beret in the Blackhorse base camp at Xuan Loc. I had been doing maintenance on my tank all day in knee-deep mud. No matter how hard you tried, that darn red mud was everywhere. After a while, we just gave up on trying to keep anything clean and only worried about changing road wheels and putting new tracks on our tanks.

After a day of this routine maintenance, Kenny Orton, a high school buddy of mine from California, came by my hooch and suggested we get something to eat at the Steak House. The Steak House, about a mile away on the other side of the base, was a small shack where you walked up to a window and placed your order for a steak dinner with french fries and a beer for five bucks. The steaks were pretty good, once you had put enough ketchup on them. The best thing though was sitting at picnic tables on the patio and enjoying your dinner and listening to the latest, popular stateside music via a reel-to-reel player.

Kenny and I were having a good time talking and watching the brilliant orange sunset slowly turn into darkness. I was also scoping out a small group of soldiers near us. In the 'Nam, you always looked for a familiar face. I noticed two men sitting over by the corner of the patio wearing black berets. I knew that soldiers from special units wore colored berets such as the better-known green berets of the Special Forces and the black berets worn by the Army Rangers.

I looked over at Kenny and asked, "What do you think those Rangers are doing here?"

Kenny shook his head indicating that he didn't know either and suggested we go over and ask them. So that's what we did.

As we got closer to them, we could see that one was a specialist fourth class (E4) and the other was a staff sergeant (E6). The sergeant actually looked to be like the younger of the two.

"Are you guys Rangers?" I asked.

"No we're ARPs." they said, laughing.

"What's an ARP?" I replied innocently.

"Sit down, buy us a beer, and we'll tell you," they said smiling.

ARPs, as it turned out, was short for Aero Rifle Platoon, an all-volunteer special infantry unit of the Air Cavalry Troop. It was formed by the commander of the 11th Armored Cavalry Regiment, Col. George S. Patton III, to replaced the former LRPs (Long Range Reconnaissance Platoon). Col. Patton was a West Point graduate and tanker just like his father, the renowned World War II general. He wanted to change the fighting tactics of the regiment and believed a larger, elite group to was necessary to accomplish this.

The sergeant told us the outfit was comprised entirely of soldiers from within the regiment and that it didn't matter what your job was because you'd be retrained. The ARPs were comprised of twenty-eight men plus a platoon sergeant and a platoon leader. This young kid sitting next to me was Staff Sergeant Rollie Port, the platoon sergeant. I was told the mission of the ARPs was two-fold. One was to go into suspected hostile areas and make contact with the enemy. If they were found, the regiment would then send in ACAVs and M48 tanks to overrun and defeat them. Their second mission was to find and recover our downed pilots.

I didn't know what Kenny was thinking, but this outfit sounded pretty cool to me. Rollie told us the ARPs were looking for a few more good men and we could request a transfer if we were interested in joining. However, we would still have to go through a series of tests and be approved by the platoon leader and the rest of the platoon before we could be fully accepted as ARPs.

During the long walk back to our own area and with the beer doing most of the talking, Kenny and I decided we wanted to join the ARPs. First thing the next morning, hangover and all, I walked into the orderly room and with only a slight hesitation requested a transfer to the ARPs.

Two weeks later, I found myself standing in the Air Cavalry Troop orderly room with my duffel bag in tow. Kenny wasn't there, though, because his commander had turned down his request. I think it broke his heart as he really wanted to be there with me. There were four of us new guys and Frank Saracino from Colorado was assigned as my roommate.

At six the next morning, we started on the first leg of our journey to becoming ARPs. We were taken to a small section of jungle within the base camp and for the next few days were trained in the intricate infantry tactics of jungle warfare. Being an ARP meant being a team player. We knew what was expected of us and learned the risks and the rewards. Our morale was always very high and I loved the training.

Each member of the four seven-man squads had to learn every job, from walking point to carrying the radio to bringing up the rear. We had to learn how to call in artillery and air strikes and a thousand other things. Each man was a part of the whole.

Our uniforms were also different from the rest of the regiment. We wore the same AK vests as our enemy. They were made of canvas, wrapped around our chests and carried our thirty-round magazines in the front three pouches. There was also room for our cleaning rods, first-aid packet, and grenades. It was lightweight and provided us with a little extra protection up front.

At first, our headgear was normally a jungle hat or the signature beret, but later on they made us wear our steel pots or at least we were told to carry them with us. We didn't like wearing those. Even though we knew they protected us better, they were just too cumbersome.

I loved being an ARP and was proud to wear that black beret! The day I stood in formation and was presented with it was the proudest day of my entire Army career. It even surpassed the day some fourteen years later when I was promoted to Chief Warrant Officer. However, holding that beret in my hand did not make me an ARP. There was a price to be paid for that honor. Would I be able to do that? Would I truly become an ARP and at what cost? You can decide if the price was too high as you read the next few stories. Don't get me wrong, I was scared as hell many times while doing this job, but I still wouldn't have traded it for the world. It was awesome serving with an all-volunteer unit. We were exceptional at our job, had a lot of pride and showed it. We were respected by all who knew us and by other units who just knew of us.

It took a certain type of man to be an ARP. It took a dedicated professional soldier who had to be just a bit crazy and knew it. At least that was the consensus of opinion among the majority of the troopers within the regiment. It was always the same comment, "If we get into a firefight, so be it. But you guys go out there everyday looking for it! You ARPs must be crazy! I'd never do that!"

That is the reason why only thirty men out of entire 11th Armored Cavalry Regiment had the honor of wearing the black beret.

ARPs My First Mission

After Sergeant Frank Saracino and I had completed our few days of intense in-house training, our platoon sergeant, Staff Sergeant Port, decided we were ready to join the ARPs on their next mission, Operation Atlas Wedge. I was assigned to the third seven-man squad and Frank was in the second. I was hoping we could both be in the same squad, but the platoon sergeant didn't want two new guys together. Because we shared a room, Frank and I had become pretty close during training. We would spent a lot of nights just lying in our bunks talking.

On the morning of our first mission, Frank was to be walking in the point man position, which meant he would be in the front of his squad. I was informed by Specialist Fourth Class Jarvis, my squad leader, that my position was to be walking backup. That would be right behind Groucho who was the third squad's best point man.

It was still dark as Frank and I sat in our room doing a final check of all our equipment. We were talking nervously about the weather as I once more checked out my CAR 15 rifle. Deep inside, I was scared but I didn't want Frank to know that. I had been in Vietnam over nine months and had already been in a few hairy firefights, but I'd always had the protection of my tank to help me feel safe. This time I'd be going into combat as a grunt protected only by jungle uniform!

It's funny because while I was scared, I was at the same time very excited. Talk about butterflies in your stomach! I sort of laughed and said to Frank, "Do you realize we're the only ARPs up in the middle night getting ready?"

He just laughed and loaded his magazines with ammunition. In the back of my mind, I knew I would have to prove myself today if I expected to earn the position of squad leader in the future.

Two hours later, we all met outside the mess hall. Everybody was joking around, but I just sort of stood back. I found my squad, but didn't know what to talk about. I surely didn't want to sound like a know-it-all.

67

Soon Jarvis came up to me. "Let's check you out, Jack, before we leave," he said looking over my gear. I tried to look as cool as I could, hoping he couldn't see my legs shaking. We broke into our own squads and walked to the chopper pad.

On the way over I looked back at Frank and hollered, "See you later, good buddy!"

He smiled and waved back. "We'll have a cold one tonight, Jack."

I started to feel a little better as I boarded the Huey. Each squad had their own Huey as well as a Loach and a Cobra gunship that escorted our platoon everywhere. They were our eyes in the sky. Those two ships together were called a "pink team." They got that name because in the Air Cavalry Troop the Loach was classified under the White Team and the Cobra under the Red. I don't exactly know why or how the different "teams" worked, all I knew is that red and white made pink.

The pink team took off first then our four Hueys lifted up and hovered above the heli-pad. The tail of our chopper kicked up while at the same time the nose went down. I could hear the jet engine roar as our ship swiftly moved down the runway. As we lifted into the air, I thought to myself, *Let's do it!*

We flew low over the treetops and I could see the farmers and their water buffalo working the fields below. The ride was so tranquil as I watched the scenery slowly drift by. It would have been really nice if I didn't know for a fact we were going into a suspected enemy stronghold. I tried to relax a little. I couldn't see our pink team, but I could hear our pilots talking with them. They were now flying over our LZ (landing zone) trying to draw fire from the enemy if he was down there in the thick jungle and rubber plantation that was to be our search area for today.

"We're getting ready to land. When we touch down, you unass this ship fast and stay behind me!" Jarvis ordered.

I nodded my head in agreement. Within minutes, our four ships dropped from the peaceful sky and rocketed into a small clearing in the jungle. The ARPs were on the ground and I did exactly as I was told. I ran like hell behind Jarvis.

68

The squads met up just outside a small hamlet on the outskirts of a very large rubber plantation. I later learned it was the Michelin Rubber Plantation and was owned by a French family. The trees in the jungle around us were layered one on top of each other so thick you couldn't see the sky above.

As we walked through the hamlet, we spotted a few chickens and small pigs, but no people. *I guess they're out working with the rubber trees.*

I was feeling pretty relaxed as we entered the front of the plantation. Our platoon broke in half with the first and second squads taking the left side and the third and fourth squads taking the right. Our pink team was still flying overhead, but we couldn't see them. We only heard them going back and fourth trying to locate a target for us.

We moved forward slowly as the point men took the lead. I was walking ten feet behind Groucho and straining my eyes to detect any movement around us. Our platoon leader, Captain White, was talking to our pilots over the radio as we moved deeper into the trees.

This place looked a lot like an orange grove except all the trees had notches cut into them and wooden pegs tapped into their bark. Small buckets hung from the pegs catching the raw rubber that was dripping into them. Man, did that shit stink! It was the worst smelling stuff I'd ever been exposed to in my life. The more seasoned guys just laughed at me as I tried to cover my nose.

About a quarter of the way into the plantation, Groucho signaled us to stop as he looked beyond the rubber trees and into the dense, six-foot tall jungle bushes in front of us. Groucho had a sixth sense and could smell the enemy before seeing them. We could see two squads to our left, twenty feet ahead of us. Capt. White was calling them over the radio to slow down when we heard a very loud and very close POP, POP, POP! It was the sound of a large caliber machine gun and it was firing in our direction! By the time I realized what it was, we were being sprayed with both rifle and light machine gun fire. We hit the ground.

Oh shit was all I could think as this once quiet grove of trees was now a solid blanket of green tracers flying in all directions from the enemy's guns. Although I was pinned to ground, I returned fire. I couldn't see anybody, so I just fired into the tree line. I felt the heat of the bullets as they were flying all around me, tearing at my clothes. I heard the platoon sergeant yell for us to find some cover. I reloaded my rife and searched for cover, but there wasn't any.

I looked for Groucho and found him fifteen feet to my left front. He was lying behind a fallen tree stump and I could see the bullets ricocheting around him. I saw the heel on of one of his boots had been blown off! He couldn't move an inch in any direction without being hit.

Someone yelled that the second squad had a person down. The captain hollered we had to get Groucho out of there and move to the rear where we could find some cover. Oddly, I no longer felt any fear as adrenaline had kicked in. I reloaded again and tried to locate the source of the green tracers. I yelled back to Jarvis and pointed to where I thought the majority of the fire was coming from. He and two other ARPs crawled forward as best they could and all four of us opened up. We must have been close because for a few seconds, the enemy fire stopped. At least it stopped long enough for Groucho to jump back to the safety of our small group.

All of the third and fourth squads were now able to very slowly crawl backward away from this killing zone. We tried to lay down as much M60 machine gun fire as we could and we leapfrogged by twos to the rear. If I hadn't been so caught up in the action, I might have enjoyed the light show from the mixture of the enemy's green tracers and our own red tracers as they covered the jungle floor.

We then set up a better and more controlled base and were now able to position our own machine guns to cover a much wider area. Our M79 grenade launchers were now hitting around the enemy with a POP-CRACK as they tore at the jungle brush. The captain knew we had to rescue the guys in the first and second squads and he was busy trying to get help from our choppers above. They said they could just barely see the smoke from the rifle fire floating above the jungle and that they, too, were receiving heavy fire from the ground. *Holy shit, what in the hell had we run into?* We regrouped to help the other two squads. We received word from them that they had been able to move back a short distance but had to leave one KIA behind. It was my new friend and roommate Frank! I just said, "Goddamn it," and reached down to load another magazine of ammunition. Wiping the tears from my eyes, I tried to focus on another target.

Capt. White said a company of First Cavalry infantry soldiers had been diverted from their mission, were already in the air, and would be at our landing zone in fifteen minutes. He instructed Groucho, Jarvis, and me to return to the landing zone and assist them back to his location. We grabbed Wheatie, our RTO (radio operator), and took him with us. The cracking sounds of incoming bullets could be heard all around as we crawled and then ran the 200 yards back to the safety of the hamlet.

Suddenly, I heard the whistle from friendly artillery rounds flying over our heads and exploding on their targets, fifty yards in front of the pinned down ARPs. I didn't have time to think of Frank now, although I knew it could easily have been me instead of him.

Soon we were looking at the clearing that was our landing zone and saw ten choppers full of First Cavalry troopers coming to our rescue. We popped green smoke and guided the ships in under a barrage of artillery exploding only 200 yards away.

A very young second lieutenant from the First Cav came up to us and Jarvis informed him that we were pinned down under heavy fire and could sure use their help. The lieutenant just laughed and told us how the First Cavalry was here now and it was no problem for his guys!

All his men were busy dropping off their large back packs as we talked. He told us to give him one man to guide his group and for the rest of us to watch their gear until they got back. Groucho led the large group of soldiers back to our men.

I stood there dumbfounded. Jarvis and I looked at each other and at the same time said, "There's no way we're staying here," and we headed back just as soon as the infantry boys were out of sight.

The artillery had just lifted as the First Cavalry troopers reached Capt. White and our men. As the two officers spoke, small arms fire started to go off once again, only this time it was answered with at least six machine guns firing in unison. The First Cavalry lieutenant told Capt. White to have his ARPs take the far left flank and his troopers would move up the middle in force. With that, the ARPs moved out and at least seventy-five First Cavalry soldiers advanced deeper into the plantation, the roar of their weapons echoing off the trees. The jungle soon smelled of gunpowder and was covered in a smoky haze.

By the time Wheatie, Jarvis, and I got back to where we had left our guys earlier, they weren't there, just some of the First Cavalry soldiers. The rest were about thirty feet ahead in the plantation.

We went looking for Capt. White when the well-hidden enemy's 51-caliber machine cut loose again. We dove for cover as troopers of the First Cavalry dropped like flies right in front of us! I couldn't believe my eyes! A pile of at least twenty dead bodies laid only ten feet away from me. They had walked right into an ambush.

I remember this next part as if it were yesterday. I saw a medic crawl over to the pile of bodies trying to give some aid. He didn't have a rifle, only his aid bag as he tried to perform his magic. I watched helplessly as a series of bullets tore through his body, then he fell to the ground. This brave, wounded soldier then got up on his knees, looked me straight in the eyes, and pointed to where the fire was coming from. I nodded back to him that I understood and when more rounds hit and killed this young hero, I saw the smoke from the muzzle of the machine gun. I'll never forget the look on his face. He knew he was going to die, but he tried to help those wounded Cavalry guys anyway. If it was not for his selfless dedication, many more lives would have been lost because no one else could see where that machine gun was located. Even though we weren't in the same unit and I didn't know his name, this medic is a hero in my book.

I called out to Jarvis that the machine gun was dug in and hidden under a dead tree stump and for everyone in the area to direct their fire on it. The hidden gun that had been spraying death so accurately throughout the battlefield was now silent. We had blown the fuck out of it. The rest of the enemy must have moved further back out of our range and deeper inside their well-hidden bunker system because the firing came to an abrupt halt.

With artillery still heard in the far distance, we now retrieved the bodies of our fallen comrades. That young second lieutenant from the First Cavalry was lying dead on the ground.

We were regrouping as three other ARPs and I requested permission to search for Frank. Capt. White told us to be careful and also take an RTO with us. We quickly headed in the direction where the second squad had last been seen. We found Frank lying in a ditch. It looked like the enemy had tried to take his boots off and his weapon was also missing. The four of us almost religiously carried Frank off the battlefield. He had been shot in the head by the 51-caliber machine gun. He never knew what hit him.

There were four helicopters on the ground when we reached the small LZ on the other side of the hamlet. One of them had a Blackhorse patch painted on its side so we carried Frank to it. As we laid him inside, one of the pilots turned to us and said, "You'll have to take that soldier back to one of the dust-off choppers."

We looked at him and replied, "He's one of us, he's an ARP, and we want you to take him home!"

I think the pilot saw the stern look in our eyes and he talked to his superior over the headset. In a moment he told us, "We'd be proud to fly him back."

The Blackhorse Huey was just clearing the tree tops by the time we got back to the plantation. That was the last time I ever saw my friend Frank. *Fly, Frank, fly, you're leaving this hell on earth.*

It wasn't long, maybe an hour, before word was sent down to pack it up and return to base camp before it got to dark. The twenty-seven remaining ARPs headed back to the LZ and our awaiting choppers.

The flight home was very quiet. All I could hear was the POP POP POP POP of the rotor blades cutting into the wind. Nobody talked about Frank. They were already starting the process of trying to forget. That wouldn't come for me for a long time. I just leaned against the wall of the chopper completely exhausted.

At 5:00 P.M., the ARPs stood in formation and our flag was lowered to half-staff in honor of our fallen comrade, Frank Saracino. My night was spent packing up his belongings. Rollie came by to help and to see how I was doing. All I could say was, "Boy, that was one hell of a first day!" He chuckled a little and tried to cheer me up. "They're not all like that. Some days are really bad!"

We talked for a while longer until everything was packed, then he said, "I'll have somebody pick up those bags in the morning. Try to get some sleep, Jack. We're going back into Michelin in the morning."

That's another story, but right now I have to try and get some sleep. I'm really tired.

Department of the Army

Headquarters, United States Army Vietnam

APO San Francisco 96375

GENERAL ORDERS   14 MAY 1969   NUMBER 1724

AWARD OF THE DISTINGUISHED SERVICE CROSS

1. TC   320. The following AWARD is announced posthumously.

SARACINO, FRANK D JR
SSAN 521-68-6426 SERGEANT

United States Army, Air Cavalry Troop, 11th Armored Cavalry Regiment, APO 96257

Awarded: Distinguished Service Cross

Date of action: 20 March 1969

Theater: Republic of Vietnam

Back to Michelin

It was 5:00 A.M. when we loaded into our waiting choppers. Our attitude this morning was a lot more serious since we knew we were going back into the Michelin Plantation. I didn't get any sleep last night and let me just say that I really had my doubts about going out again this morning. I knew I couldn't quit even though my mind was telling me, *Jack, you're crazy. You can quit right now. You volunteered for this shit and you don't have to get on that chopper.* As I climbed onboard, I just kept telling myself that if the other guys could do it, then so could I. After all, they were as scared as I was. I just had to do it. I had to make the grade.

As our four choppers started the drop into the small LZ (landing zone) just outside the plantation, I was amazed at how different it looked this morning. There had been three bomb strikes put in here last night and many rubber trees were lying in large piles scattered throughout the plantation. The thick jungle that surrounded Michelin was now scarred with long rows of huge craters left by the 250-pound bombs. I thought to myself, *Maybe it will be okay today. How could anything or anybody survive through such bombing?* As our chopper set down in the tall elephant grass of the LZ, we all rushed to the safety of the small hamlet next to the plantation.

The ACAVs from both I & K troops were already there, along with two platoons of tanks from M company. "They must have driven all night to get here," I said to Jarvis as my squad found a good place to sit down while awaiting our orders. There had been no small talk on the flight out. I think we all had bad vibes about this place and had that all-too-familiar feeling in our guts. I can't explain it; I think you'd just have to be in a firefight to understand it.

A few minutes later, Captain White walked up to us and laid out the plans for today. The ARPs would be going back to the same area we'd been in yesterday. We'd be looking for any dead NVA (North Vietnamese Army) soldiers and any weapon caches that might still be hidden in the tunnels or bunkers. Then we'd push further north into the surrounding jungle and follow any blood trails. The ACAVs of K troop and tanks of M company would support us if needed, while the ACAVs of I troop would move along either side of the plantation to surround any NVA caught in the center. Today the ARPs were going to be the bait!

We would start at 7:00 A.M., only twenty minutes from now. Jarvis informed me that I'd be walking between the RTO (radio operator) and our rear man, Lammie-Pie. I was glad he didn't make me walk the point. No way was I ready for that position!

The four squads of ARPs had just formed up when the radio on Wheatie's back came alive with the command to move out. It was slow going as we crawled over and around many of the large burnt and still smoldering fallen trees and tried our best to maintain a straight line. We had to stop from time to time as our guys searched the many blown open and now uncovered tunnels and bunkers that had hidden and protected the enemy only yesterday.

When we reached the area where Frank had been killed, my body filled with rage. I told myself, *Today is payback day, Frank.* I looked even harder trying to see just one more live Gook.

The smell of gunpowder still hung heavy in the air as the early morning dew held the odor to the leaves and fallen trees. The memories of yesterday kept trying to come back to me as I slowly moved forward. I told myself I had to forget about it if I wanted to stay alive. I had to get back to the business at hand. I knew that I needed all of my wits about me.

What we were doing was called a search and destroy operation. It would take us almost three hours before we had finally checked out all of the bunkers and tunnels within the plantation. Although we found no weapons or dead bodies, we did find at least a dozen blood trails leading into the jungle to our immediate front.

When we reached the wall of trees leading into the jungle, we stopped and took a break while the captain decided how to proceed. It was decided we would form back into squads and enter the thick brush in a single file line, the way we usually walked on a mission.

78

We moved forward, cutting our way through the brush with our knives. Sticky branches were everywhere.

It took what seemed like forever before we finally broke into a small clearing. Wheatie, who was still in front of me, was yelling as he pulled a large sticky branch off of his back. "You know, Jack, there's got to be a better way to make a buck!" he said as he finally pulled the last thorn from his back.

"Yeah, this shit is really thick," I said and lit up a smoke. I knew that smoking was bad for you but in a place like Vietnam, that vice was pretty low on the totem pole.

We took another short break as Capt. White checked his compass readings. He located true north and then we moved about thirty feet into the thick stuff. Groucho raised his hand, stopping the squad from going any further. Jarvis started to say something when Groucho gave the sign to hit the dirt. The squad reacted without question. It was a good thing because two seconds later we were blanketed with a hail of incoming bullets!

The distinct crack of AK-47s firing had broken the silence and I found myself once again pinned down by enemy fire. I strained to see the enemy's muzzle flash in the jungle, but I couldn't see any. Bullets were flying over my head and chunks of dirt were exploding all around us. Then the NVA 30-caliber machine gun joined in. Not only were we firing our weapons, but we were also throwing hand grenades into the thickest cluster of trees to our front.

Capt. White was hollering over the radio for us to move back to the rear, but Groucho, Wheatie, and I were too close to the enemy who was no more than twenty feet away. There was no way for us to go anywhere. Every time one of our grenades exploded, the enemy machine gun would stop firing. But within seconds, it would start again.

Jarvis would holler out every so often to make sure that nobody was hurt. So far we all were okay, except for the fact that we couldn't move one way or the other and could only push some of the soft dirt around us for protection.

Groucho and I spotted the machine gun and the three men who were firing it. One of them moved into the open as he was reaching for more ammunition. Groucho hit him with his first shot and I put three more rounds into him before he hit the ground. "That's for Frank!" I hollered to Groucho as we threw two more grenades in the direction of the machine gun.

It went silent for the last time, but the heavy small arm fire was still swirling over our heads. The war had finally gotten to me, I was becoming hardened. I was glad I had gotten my payback. No matter what happened to me now, at least the debt was paid. This was war and killing came with the job.

I heard the familiar sound of ACAVs behind us. Thank God we were going to be rescued. If we could only hang in there for the next few minutes, then every thing would be all right.

The tracks were on line and about fifty yards to our rear. It was hard to see them, but just their loud noise made me feel safe and renewed my hopes in getting out of here. I yelled out to Groucho, "The ACAVs are coming! They're on the way!"

"And not a damn bit too soon either!" he snapped back.

Then the unbelievable happened. They started firing at us! I mean 50-caliber and M60 rounds were flying in our position and bullets were now hitting all around us from both sides! Strips of bark were falling on top of me as I tried to figure out what in the hell was going on. *What the fuck? Don't they know we're here?* I tried to dig myself deeper into the ground.

My mind couldn't accept what was taking place. I hollered as loud as I could to Groucho, "Holy shit, they're going to kill us! We've got to do something!"

They were now only thirty feet away from us, still firing their guns. Without thinking, and risking my own safety, I jumped up and threw my full plastic canteen as hard as I could at the closest M60 gunner. I managed to hit him right on his helmet! He didn't know what happened as he fell away from his machine gun grabbing at his helmet. That was all I needed.

I ran to the ACAV as bullets continued to fly all around me. I remember thinking how stupid I was and that there was no way that I'd ever reach that ACAV alive. But it was too late to stop. I don't know how but in one giant leap, I found myself inside the track. I

80

was standing next to a very surprised gunner whose neck I grabbed with both my hands as I screamed, "What in the fuck are you guys doing? Don't you know that you have friendly troops on the ground in front of you?!"

Next, I grabbed the track commander's shirt so hard that he almost fell over. "You guys have to cease fire! There's ARPs on the ground in front of you!"

The track commander, a young buck sergeant, yelled over his radio for K troop to cease fire, but it still took almost ten minutes before they finally stopped. The ACAVs then moved in between the ARPs and gave us time to get behind them before they started firing again. I don't know how, but not one ARP was wounded by our own guys! There must have been at least a thousand rounds that landed around us. None of us could believe the luck we had on that day.

All hell broke loose as the tracks, who were now fifty feet deeper into the jungle, started getting hit with rocket-propelled grenades. WHAM! WHAM! The two ACAVs took direct hits and started to burn. Next, an M48 tank, only thirty feet to my left, took a hit. The crew tried valiantly to fight back, but three more rockets hit them and their tank was immediately engulfed in flames.

Some of us ARPs ran to the burning tracks and pulled out as many wounded guys as we could. We looked for the safest place to put them and found a large bomb crater that would have to do. Capt. White was on the radio calling for our medics to get over to the crater and within minutes we had a mini-aid station set up.

You could hear the increased tempo of the battle as our troops fired everything they had into the tree line. Soon we had at least twenty wounded soldiers in the crater and the captain was trying to get some dust-off choppers into our area. It seemed like there were choppers of all kinds - Loaches, Hueys, and Cobras - flying overhead, swooping down low into the trees trying to locate the enemy's stronghold. Some of our guys went off to set up an emergency landing zone for the choppers.

This was the start of a very bad day for the troops of the third squadron, but I could see by the bodies of the enemy that it wasn't going to be any better for them either. I was too tired to count them, but I knew that there had to be at least sixty.

Our Cobra gunships were making low passes over our heads trying to suppress the enemy fire. The sky was now covered with a mixture of white and black smoke. Sitting in the crater, covered in sweat, I held the hand of a wounded GI. I wanted to do more, but I wasn't a medic. This guy needed me if for nothing else than to just be there. I never did know his name, but that didn't matter. I knew that he would have done the same for me, too.

As always, Major "Doc" Bahnsen, the Air Cavalry Troop commander, had been directing the aircraft overhead. I guess that he must have seen the enemy stronghold because his chopper dropped right into the middle of the firefight. In fact, the dust from his landing was so strong that I had to lie across my wounded friend to keep him safe. Then I saw Maj. Bahnsen run from his command chopper as his co-pilot, while taking hits, took the ship straight up fifty feet and then banked it hard to the left as he flew over the treetops and away from my view.

Next, the major ran over to one of the tanks, climbed onboard and rode it back into the battle. All of the other tracks moved forward and the third squadron soon destroyed the enemy stronghold. It was only another thirty minutes before almost all of the fighting stopped.

As the last of the wounded were flown out, the ARPs regrouped and started searching the battlefield. Three hours later, we were on our way back to Bien Hoa.

Operation Atlas Wedge would go on for another six days, but the ARPs' job was done. We had found the enemy and were now needed elsewhere.

Another Day in the ARPs

The story I'm about to share with you is particularly difficult for me to even think about but you paid good money to read about my escapades in Vietnam, so I'm obligated to tell you. This story has remained hidden deep within my soul, a story I still have nightmares about. This is going to be a bit graphic so if you're not up to it, please go on to another story. Ready? Let's take a trip together into the darkest side of war.

Today was going to be a great. At our morning formation, we were informed it would be a non-working day for us. This was only my third day off since I joined the unit two months earlier, so I was really excited about it. There were so many things I needed to do like get that haircut I was supposed to have gotten last week and go to the PX (post exchange) to drop off some film and pick up some more goodies to eat.

After we were released from formation, I told my squad to be sure to check in with the platoon sergeant before they left the company area. That was the policy in the ARPs. I had just been moved up to the position of squad leader of the third squad. Specialist Fourth Class Roger Jarvis had decided I was ready to take command. He had been in charge of our squad since the old squad leader was killed two months before. I really liked and respected Roger. He was a good ol' country boy who really knew his job and taught me something new on every mission.

I went back to my room to pick up some money and spotted a buddy going into his section of the hooch. "Hey, Sam!" I hollered out, "do you want to go to the PX with me?"

"Hell no, I'm not doing one damn thing today but lay on my ass and sleep!"

I took that as a no and charged out the front door looking to find Rollie Port, our platoon sergeant. It was starting to sprinkle a little, but even that wasn't going to dampen my spirits! I ran all over the company area but I couldn't find hide nor hair of Rollie anywhere.

83

Finally, I ran into two other ARPs, Pineapple and Dan Bock, and asked them if they had seen Port anywhere.

"Yeah, check in the TOC (Tactical Operations Center). I think I saw him and Captain White go in there a minute ago." they said.

I thanked them and headed to the TOC.

Capt. White was our platoon leader and a good officer. The TOC was inside a huge bunker and filled with radios that were in contact with every unit in the regiment. I never could figure out how they kept track of all of them at the same time.

I walked up to the outside, went right passed the large "Restricted Area" sign, around the triple rows of barbed, wire and finally down the wooden steps into a small dark room. There stood an MP who wanted to know what I was doing there. I asked if SSG Port was inside and the MP said he'd see. He went through a small wooden door. I could hear the radios blaring away when it opened. When Rollie stuck his head out, I could tell by the look in his eyes something was wrong.

"Get the guys saddled up, Jack, we got a chopper just go down near Dong Nai. Tell the men I want them at the chopper pad in twenty minutes! No later!" Then he ducked back into the room. *Well, there goes my day off!* I thought as I ran up the stairs and out into the daylight.

I rushed in the front door of our squad leader's hooch and yelled, "There's a chopper down! Get your guys to the pad!" I went out the back door and headed toward the hooch my squad lived in. There was no complaining this day. It was our pilots who were on the ground. These were the guys who covered our butts and we knew we had to get there fast if they were to live. In fifteen minutes, all twenty-eight of us ARPs were loading into Hueys and our pink team was already clearing the runway.

On the flight out, we were told a Loach had gone down with two men on board. The pilots also told me it was going to be a hot LZ (a landing zone where the enemy is firing at the choppers) and that four gunships were working the area right now. This was to be my first time going into a known hot LZ. My butt was already puckered up when I told my squad what was going on. I was scared

84

shitless! I knew I had to keep my cool in order to keep my squad alive. My adrenaline was pumping like crazy!

As we approached the crash sight, I could see the smoke from the burning Loach and also from the rockets being fired by the Cobra gunships. I hollered to my men to get ready as our ship dropped out of the sky and into the range of the guns of our enemies below. We were taking hits even though our door gunners were putting out as much firepower as they could. We still had over twenty feet before we could unload from this immense target.

Bullets exploded all around us as we jumped as fast as we could from the Huey and ran toward the first sign of cover we could find. We made it! We were now on the ground! Now the ARPs would take charge of this small plot of jungle.

The terrain around us was nothing more than a bombed out portion of jungle. The trees had been blown to bits and there was nothing left but huge chunks of treetops scattered about like Tinkertoys on a kid's bedroom floor. The ground was covered with large craters filled with dark-brown, thick, gooey mud and surrounded by thick jungle foliage, some still green but most already burnt to a brownish color.

We were all firing our weapons as we attempted to group together. The incoming fire wasn't as intense now because the VC could no longer see us as well as they did when we were in the chopper. I could see a small cluster of brush to our right front that had at least two VC firing from beneath its base. My squad directed all our fire into that lone bush and completely demolished both it and the two soldiers who had been hiding there.

We then moved forward, slowly working our way deeper into the thickest area of the jungle. Again, we received incoming fire. The enemy's green tracers were hitting all around us tearing chunks of bark from the fallen trees while some of the rounds were going deep into the mud with a THUNK as they hit. We continued firing at anything that moved.

I was completely covered in mud by now and was slipping all around as I tried to get out of that damn crater I'd just fallen into!

Wheatie, my radio operator, yelled over to me, "Hey, Jack, Rollie wants us to catch up and get our asses up with the other guys."

"Tell him we're doing the best we can and we'll be there in a minute," I replied.

I finally climbed out of the water-filled crater and jumped over to Jarvis. He pointed and said, "Lets go through this way. Lay down some cover for me and I'll take two of the guys with me." Then he and two others stood up and ran around some of the blown down tree stumps leaping right between two bushes that were at least eight feet tall.

The rest of us provided cover fire until I heard Jarvis call out. "We made it through. I can see the chopper!" The rest of the platoon had gone around the other way and were now almost to where Jarvis and my other two men were lying.

I yelled back to Jarvis, "Cover us, buddy. We're coming in!" When I heard their guns firing, the remaining three ARPs and I jumped headfirst into this thick brush.

Our gunships were busy flying overhead trying to draw the enemy fire away from us. Every time one of the VC fired at our choppers meant we ARPs had another target. And that meant one more dead VC! There had to be at least twenty of them by now.

It seemed like we'd been on the ground for hours, but it had only been about forty minutes. My squad was now within thirty yards of our objective, a small two-man helicopter called a Loach. It was completely burnt and dense black smoke was pouring out of what was once the crew compartment. I tried to locate the missing pilots but I couldn't see them from where we were. We had to get closer. I radioed to Rollie and was told to stay put until the other three squads could get to us. The Loach was in the middle of a small clearing. It looked as if the pilots had tried to land their ship as best they could until they were blown apart by the intense enemy ground fire.

Within minutes, all of the squad leaders were talking with Capt. White over the radios and a plan was soon decided upon. My squad would go to the chopper while the other squads would circle the downed Loach and provide us with cover fire. At the same time, we were going to get some artillery to drop in around us. Maybe that would keep the VCs' heads down long enough for us to get the pilots out.

It took ten minutes before we heard the shells flying over head. During that time, the enemy had increased their fire in our direction as they were attempting to come in for the kill. But as the first rounds exploded to our front, we could see a few dead VC being thrown in the air by the blast.

Capt. White gave the command to move out and the seven men of my squad crawled on our bellies through the mud toward the still burning ship. It took us five minutes to cover the thirty yards. I will never forget the horror I saw next. Our two pilots were lying side by side next to their chopper. They were both burnt to death, their bodies still smoldering with portions of their flight suits melted to their bodies. The VC had tried to remove their boots. A 38-caliber pistol lay next to one of them, its barrel bent in half from the impact of the crash. You could hardly tell these two bodies were once men they were burnt so badly. These two poor souls were now just crispy pieces of burnt meat. I started to get the dry heaves. I wanted to vomit but couldn't. I had a job to do. I had to get these two young pilots out of here. I had to get all of us out of here!

This was only the second time I'd ever been real close to our own dead. The troops around me acted in the same manner as the one time before, handling our fallen comrade with dignity and respect. Even with enemy bullets hitting all around, we took our time. With silent honor, we carefully wrapped each body in a poncho. It was like for a brief moment everything around us just stopped. I couldn't hear my men, the radio, or any of the sounds of war as I completed the horrible task I'd been given.

Body parts were falling off as we lifted the bodies onto the ponchos. We put each limb back into place and covered them as best we could. My squad then tried to lift them up, but they were just too heavy for us. Each pilot must have now weighed close to 300 pounds. Jarvis cut down two tree limbs to put through the plastic ponchos. "I've seen this before, Jack," he said. Burned bodies are really heavy. We're going to have a hard time carrying these guys out."

Between the artillery and the cover fire, we managed to get the two pilots to a clearing about a thousand yards away. It took us almost an hour to get there. We were all exhausted and even had to drag the poor pilots for the last twenty feet. The smell of burnt flesh had finally gotten the best of me and as we laid our pilots on the ground, I fell to my knees and vomited on the jungle floor. I didn't care if anybody saw me or not. Some things are just too much for any man to handle and this was one of them.

The tide of battle had turned as the exploding rounds were taking their toll on the VC. The rest of the ARPs soon joined us and we prepared to evacuate our two dead friends. I had been around many dead soldiers before and will be after today, but I will never forget that horrid smell. I can't even begin to describe it to you. There are no words know to man to describe that odor.

Within the hour we were all on our choppers flying home. No ARP had been killed or wounded this day and we received no ground fire as we lifted off. I think the enemy was too busy picking up their thirty or more dead and cussing out the men who wore the Blackhorse patch. If this was what it's like to have a day off, I'd just as soon work every day until I got home!

Thanks for letting me share my nightmare. After thirty years, maybe I'll now be able to sleep through the night. I still to this day do not know the names of those two brave pilots. I only remember their faces.

A Surprise For Charlie

It was early evening when Staff Sergeant Rollie Port, our young platoon sergeant, gathered the four squad leaders of the ARPs in the NCO hooch and gave us an operations order.

"We're going into a suspected North Vietnamese Army bunker complex in the morning. Be ready at 0700 hours," was all he had to say.

"Shit, Rollie I'm leaving for Hawaii in only two days! I thought we'd stay in base camp until then," I said.

"So did I," he replied, "but when the troop commander says go, we go."

"Yeah, I know, I was just getting myself psyched up." I said disappointedly. Rollie told us to be sure and inform our guys.

Back at our area I found Wheatie returning from the showers and asked if he knew where the rest of our squad was.

"They all went over to the NCO Club, Jack. Do you want to walk there with me?"

I thought why not, I could use one of those nasty tasting burgers and a beer. "Sure, Wheatie, I'll wait on you while you get ready." Soon we were walking to the largest NCO Club in Bien Hoa.

It belonged to the 101st Airborne Division, the famous "Screaming Eagles," but anyone could use it. Sometimes on Saturday night, a fight would break out between the guys from the 101st and the 11th Cavalry troopers, usually over whose unit was the best. There was always enough security to stop it before it got to far out of hand.

It was Friday, so I figured there would be some sort of band playing. There usually was one on Friday and Saturday nights. They were never very good but you could always count on them to be very loud! As we got closer to the club, we could hear them.

Once inside, we could see it was really packed. We were headed to a small counter to put our food order in when I spotted our guys sitting at a table in the back of the room. I walked over to them thinking how awful this South Korean band sounded. After a few beers, however, I'd be singing right along with the others who'd already joined in with this terrible sounding foursome.

"Hi, guys. Guess what? We're going out in the morning." I announced.

"Oh, shit!" they moaned in unison. They, too, had been expecting to have tomorrow off.

"Pull up a seat, we might as well party tonight," Jarvis said pointing to two empty chairs. "Tomorrow's just another day."

I reached over to shake the hand of my good friend, Bruce. He was also in the ARPs, but in a different squad. I can't think of any of the twenty-eight ARPs who I didn't like.

I went to get my food and returned to find a cold beer waiting for me. "Nice ass!" Groucho yelled to one of the Korean girls dancing on the stage. One of our guys answered back with, "They all look nice to you, Groucho!" The poor girl on stage was trying to do her best imitation of a go-go dancer but just couldn't seem to get it all together. Nobody could do it as well as an American girl!

We spent the next couple of hours smoking and joking, but when the band stopped for the night, it was time for us to leave. After all, we did have a mission in the morning. We walked back to our hooches in single file, the way we did in the jungle. As I was walking along the dark road, I was thinking how much I really enjoyed myself tonight. It was nice to take a break from the reality of our surroundings. We had partied a little too hard and drunk a little too much, but that too was the way it was in the 'Nam. Everything was pushed to the limits because we knew it could all end tomorrow.

The next morning came way too early for me but I did manage to get my squad and myself to the chopper pad on time. We lifted off at 7:00 and by 8:30 were already setting down at the landing zone, hangovers and all.

After walking through the jungle for about twenty minutes, we arrived at our objective, a well-hidden old bunker complex. We searched that damn thing from top to bottom but didn't find a thing. Not even an old can of sardines was to be found anywhere! That was the favorite food of the NVA soldiers and would always be present if they were anywhere around the area.

It had to be over one hundred degrees as we climbed in and out of the many tunnels and bunkers covering over a click (thousand square meters) that was our search area for today. I was especially happy when we finally got the word to pack it up and head for home. I'd be getting on a plane for Hawaii the next morning after all!

All the guys were hot, tired, and thinking only of a cold shower followed by a cold brew when we loaded into our four awaiting choppers. We still had to travel the forty minutes back to base camp before we could taste that cold one waiting for us. Jarvis and the boys were a little depressed about how the mission had gone and our adrenaline was still pumping. It always took a few hours to settle down and get back to normal.

The pilots from the Air Cavalry Troop were flying us over the main highway between Xuan Loc and Bien Hoa. They were using this main artery between the two cities as a guide to take us home. I was sitting near the door of the chopper, relaxing as I watched the traffic move along the highway below. I was thinking how small they looked down there. The popping of the rotor blades was the only sound I heard.

As I looked along the road, I could see the tail end of a long convoy slowly winding its way toward Bien Hoa. The majority of this stretch of highway looked the same - a two-lane blacktop road with fifty yards of cleared, grassy open areas on both sides and heavy jungle beyond that. It reminded me of the many hours I had spent on this same road with M company. We had spent many a day pulling convoy security in our tanks. It was boring work, but was necessary to keep our boys safe while they delivered supplies that were much needed by the troops.

All of a sudden the copilot turned to me and said, "The convoy is getting attacked! Hold on and get ready, we're going in!"

Our chopper came alive, picking up speed. "Oh shit, here we go again!" I said out loud alerting my men who were trying to see below. Our pink team of Loach and Cobra helicopters were already making their attack. They were flying low and fast toward the rear of the convoy, their guns already finding their targets far ahead of us. The Cobra had large clouds of smoke coming from the tail section as its deadly rockets were firing into the thick jungle to the left of the convoy.

Apparently, a group of at least sixty VC guerillas fired RPGs (rocket propelled grenades) from the jungle brush on the north side and were now running toward the convoy, firing rifles on the way to the jungle on their south. They must have been dinky-dau (crazy)!

Our chopper was now coming in fast with the door gunners firing all around the wounded convoy. Any ARP who could find a target was also firing. The VC were almost inside of the convoy and at least four trucks were now burning out of control. The black smoke from the fires was starting to cloud our view.

Our four choppers hovered directly over the tops of the burning trucks firing at the enemy ten feet below us. Gooks were running in every direction when they realized their attack wasn't going to be as successful as they'd planned. The majority of the VC had already crossed through the convoy and were now headed toward the safety of the jungle that was fifty yards to the south. Our ships set down in the grass next to the burning convoy long enough for us to jump off, then they took off again.

Our medic headed in the direction of the burning trucks, looking for any wounded drivers. The ARPs were now on line and firing in the direction of the fleeing enemy. It was like a turkey shoot as we laid down as much firepower as we could. It didn't take long before the tall grass was burning from the heat of our bullets. The gunners from the four Hueys hovering twenty feet above us were working their bullets along the southern tree line. Meanwhile, our gunships were searching the northern portion of the jungle for any more VC who might be trying to get away. A few of the truck drivers were now helping us and we moved forward in the tall grass trying to locate any still alive or hiding VC.

This whole operation took less then twenty minutes but I was totally exhausted! I reloaded for the fourth time and started firing single shots. I could tell we had them licked. Not one VC could have made it back into the jungle.

The convoy had lost six trucks and one jeep, but thank God only two men. Three more were wounded. It could have been so much worse than that. The boys in that convoy sure won't forget that day or the men from the ARPs either.

I checked on my squad once more before we loaded into the choppers for what I hoped would be a nonstop flight back to base camp. While in the air, I couldn't help but think there would be a few less guys in the club tonight. We all knew we were expendable and in a week's time the club would be full once again. Would this war ever end? Hawaii, here I come!

Night Ambush

It was 5:30 A.M. when I walked into the enlisted hooch to make sure my guys were getting up. I spotted Wheatie sitting on his bunk singing along with some country song on the radio. When I got closer I asked him, "Wheatie, what did you do with all the money?"

He turned around, looked at me and asked, "What money, Sarge?"

I knew I had him then. "The money your Mom gave you for singing lessons!"

I was laughing at my own joke when one of the other guys hollered out, "That sounds like something my Dad would say!" They all started laughing.

I walked out the front door and headed for the mess hall. As the morning sun hit me in the face, I thought, *Damn, that was something my Dad used to say to me, too!* After breakfast, my squad and I met Captain White at the chopper pad. We were going to a small plantation that was two miles east of the infamous Michelin rubber plantation where we'd made contact with the enemy before. This time we would be supporting K troop of the third squadron. They were going to search a small section of jungle that was suspected having been used by the North Vietnamese Army during the past week.

What I thought was going to be cool was that a team of mine-sniffing dogs was going to be there as well. They were going to check out the main roads that criss-crossed all the smaller plantations. I'd never worked with the dogs before and was excited about watching them in action. I had a feeling this was going to be one of those good days!

Staff Sergeant Homer "Pops" Hungerford, our new platoon sergeant, was yelling at us to get on board so my squad headed for our chopper that was warming up. Everybody seemed really relaxed, as if this was going to be just another day in the 'Nam. As I climbed into the chopper, I yelled out over the roar, "Good morning, Pops! How they hanging today?" He gave me one of his

95

annoyed looks. I always enjoyed this part, when the choppers first took off and we picked up speed and then shot down the runway.

We normally followed the river out of Bien Hoa. The rice paddies along the riverbank always looked so green to me. After about ten minutes, though, we would bank off and head toward the countryside and the uncertainties of the jungle that lay just beyond.

Since this is going to be at least a forty-five minute flight and since you can only look at so much jungle before getting bored, I'll tell you about our new platoon sergeant. Pops has had quite an interesting past so let me relate a few stories.

About a month ago, SSG Rollie Port, our then platoon sergeant, moved up to the TOC (Tactical Operations Center) to work until he went home in two months and SSG Hungerford was assigned as our new platoon sergeant. He was forty-two years old. That was almost twice my age! Rumor had it he had served in World War II as a sergeant, in the Korean Conflict as an officer, and was now in Vietnam as a sergeant again. Something was said about him being in the reserves. I didn't really understand all that stuff, but I immediately liked SSG Hungerford and soon, because of his age, "Pops" became his nickname. He accepted it with pride.

What I liked best about Pops were the long talks we used to have. Since he had served in similar outfits as my Dad and had been stationed at many of the same Army posts, we would spend hours talking about the good old days.

I can recall shortly after he arrived, we were on one of his first missions and were taking enemy fire. We couldn't see the Viet Cong through the dense foliage, but we were still firing short burst from our rifles until we all could move back to a safer place. I was pinned down pretty good and every time I tried to move around, another bullet whizzed out of nowhere and soared past my head. The Viet Cong had me zeroed in and I thought for sure that I was going to die.

As I rolled on my side to load another magazine into my rifle, I noticed Pops about twenty feet to my rear appearing altogether unconcerned about the bullets flying around us. As a matter of fact, he was leaning against a small tree eating from a can of peaches!

I yelled back to him, "Pops, what the hell you doing? We're getting shot at!"

He yelled back, "When I see 'em, I'll shoot 'em! Right now it's my lunchtime."

On another occasion, we were clearing out an old bunker system. The guys were throwing grenades inside so they would collapse and be of no further use to the VC. Well, Pops was standing over a hole about to toss in a grenade when Specialist Fourth Class Bruce Stephens spotted him.

As Pops was yelling, "Fire in the hole!" Bruce yelled out as loud as he could, "Pops, don't throw that grenade, it's a shitter!" Bruce ran over to where Pops was standing and stopped him. If Pops had tossed a grenade in that hole, everyone within fifty yards would have been covered from head to toe with shit!

Well, back to our mission. As I turned and looked out the chopper door, I could see about twenty ACAVs (armored cavalry assault vehicles) down below. That's got to be K troop waiting for us. I'll have to tell you more about Pops later, but right now hang on 'cause we're going in!

I could see the cloud of yellow smoke the guys from K troop had popped for our pilots. I always felt sorry for the poor guy who had to guide in our ships. He had to stand in the middle of the landing zone with his hands up over his head and stay there until the first Huey hovered directly in front of him. Then he put his hands out to his side, which was the signal for the Huey to set down on the ground. That lone soldier would get completely covered in dirt and whatever else was stirred up by the instant windstorm created by the chopper blades.

Once we were on the ground, the four choppers took off and we walked to the center of the K troop's perimeter. I was looking around trying to find some of my buddies. Capt. White would be reporting to the troop commander and that meant we had at least fifteen minutes to goof off. I could see the dogs and their handlers not far away and headed in that direction. Hell, I could see my friends anytime, but not the dogs!

They were big dogs, German shepherds, I think. Their handlers said they really could smell out a mine. I was busy petting one of them when Pops yelled for me to join the other ARPs. I guess my fifteen-minute break was over.

The game plan was for the first and second squads to go with the dog teams and provide security for them, while my squad and the fourth squad would push up ahead and check out the narrow bridges and the plantation area in general. I had really wanted to watch the dogs in action but that was not to be, so I started down the road with my guys.

We were about 200 yards ahead of the dogs when I heard the ACAVs fire up their engines. They were going to follow the dog teams down the road until they could branch off into the small plantations along both sides of the road. It would be their job to find any bunkers that might be located within the groves of rubber trees.

It didn't take more than thirty minutes before the dogs had sniffed out their first buried mine. The call came over the radio for us to hold up where we were until the mine was uncovered. My squad was stopped next to a stone bridge, so I sat down on one of the large rocks and told my guys to take a break. I sat there and pouted about not being able to see the dogs in action.

I was looking out through the grove of trees on the left side of the road when I spotted three of the K troopers about a hundred yards inside of the plantation. It looked like they were laying out communication wire because they had a rather large spool with them. It struck me as a little odd, but I smiled and waved at them. "What are you guys doing way over there?" I called to them.

At first they waved back, but then suddenly they looked at each other, dropped the wire and ran like hell! I tried to get a better look at them by putting my hand above my eyes. One of them had on a tan uniform and was wearing a pith helmet! "Shit, they're NVA!" I screamed as I lifted my rifle to my shoulder. I fired off about twenty rounds in their direction. It didn't take long for Jarvis to see what was going on and in only seconds we were both covering the area with small arms fire.

The radio on Wheatie's back came alive as our captain wanted to know what the hell was going on. Wheatie told him we had spotted three NVA soldiers inside the plantation and were shooting at them. Well, that's not true. Actually what he really said was, "We're shooting at the fuckers, sir!" but I won't say that.

"Hold your fire until I can get there," was the next thing out of the radio. It took Capt. White and Pops about two minutes to reach our location as they scrambled on a dead run.

"Are you sure you saw NVA soldiers, Jack?" the captain asked.

"Sure I'm sure, sir".

"Okay, third and fourth squads, let's get on line and see if we can find anything. Keep your eyes open." the captain ordered as our small group began to move slowly through the plantation.

Sure enough, we found one dead NVA soldier next to the large spool of communications wire and within twenty minutes, the fourth squad had literally uncovered an NVA colonel. He had been hiding in a small hole in the ground camouflaging himself with bamboo over his head.

Excited, Capt. White said, "Good job, guys! Now let's get this man back to the K troop commander."

My squad and I went back to the bridge and waited for further orders. Talk about an rush!

I don't really know why this next decision was made, but about a half an hour later we were told to keep working the road with the dog team and the ACAVs would be going on ahead to search the plantation. Well, they couldn't use the road because it hadn't been cleared of mines yet, so they spread out between the rubber trees, got themselves on line, and slowly rolled forward. They only had five ACAVs on line because this section of the plantation was very narrow.

It took K troop a while to get set up as they brought in extra men to load onto their five tracks. They now had a commander behind the 50-caliber gun and two side gunners, each standing behind their M60 machine guns, and the two extra men riding up on top behind the two M60 guys. Their job was to look for any signs of tunnel openings. The closest track was only thirty feet away from me. I'll

99

never forget its name, "The Ace of Spades." I figured that had something to do with the fact that the crew was all black. They were getting closer to me so I waved and yelled to them, "Give 'em hell, guys!" That was about the same time they ran over the 250-pound mine.

First I saw the flash and the dust from the explosion, then I watched the track shake and jump straight up in the air at least five feet. Finally came the thundering, ear-shattering sound of the blast. I had my eyes pinned on the soldier who had been sitting on the rear of the "Ace Of Spades." He had been blown straight up another ten feet above the already airborne ACAV. This poor scared soldier was trying to run in midair! His legs and arms were moving like crazy and he turned his head to look at me. His eyes were as big as saucers when he started to slowly descend into the giant cloud of dust that now consumed the whole track.

When he hit the ground, his feet didn't skip a beat and he ran off into the plantation like he'd been shot out of a cannon. I mean for that moment, he was the fastest man on earth. He was literally flying through the thick smoke and dust until he ran out of my sight deep within the plantation. I couldn't help but chuckle at the whole scene. Thankfully, about five minutes later, he came walking back to his blown up track still shaking his head in disbelief.

You're not going to believe this, but within minutes of the explosion, another track, the one on the other side, also hit a mine! K troop was beginning to have a really bad day. Needless to say, not a single track moved until the dogs had checked for hidden mines. The whole place was nothing but one big minefield and clearing it would take the rest of the day.

Pops gathered the ARPs together and told us we'd be here at least another day. He also said that because of what they'd found out from the captured NVA colonel, we now knew that one battalion of the 274th VC Regiment was working this area. More ACAVs from I & L troops and the tanks of M company would be here in the morning. Pops also said we were going out on night ambush and that our extra gear would arrive on the chow chopper later. I don't know about you, but it sounded like we were getting deeper into it again!

Capt. White said the first and second squads would work with the dog teams until dark, which was in about three hours, and the third and fourth squads would be pulling the night ambush along with SSG Hungerford. We were told to relax for the next few hours, so I found a nice shaded spot and just cooled it.

About an hour had passed before the two M88 recovery tracks showed up looking for the two damaged ACAVs. I knew one of the track commanders from my tanker days so I went along with them to help. Later, my friends, Bruce and Dan, from the first squad told me those dogs had uncovered fifteen mines in a one-acre area.

We ate dinner, which consisted of pork slices with gravy (that ran off the sides of your plate and destroyed anything it landed on), mashed potatoes, corn, and two slices of bread. A meal fit for a king. Next we unpacked the overnight boxes that carried trip flares, claymores, ponchos, and some extra ammunition for the M60 machine guns. It was almost dark and within the hour we'd be headed to our ambush sight. Night ambush wasn't bad if you were on your own, but it always made me a little nervous if we were working close to your own troops. The last thing I wanted was to get caught in crossfire.

It took us thirty minutes to reach the ambush position which was located next to a well-traveled foot trail. It was about 300 yards due south of K troop's night defensive position and sat between two of the smaller groves of rubber trees. It was the perfect place to catch the enemy moving along this narrow path linking the three-mile chain of rubber plantations.

We laid out trip flares, some on both ends of the narrow footpath and some running the length of the jungle across our front. There was now a total of eight trip wires (not much thicker than heavy-duty thread) protecting our front and both of our flanks. The rear of our ambush sight was so thick with brush that we didn't need to put anything back there. Next came fourteen claymore mines, one to be detonated by each man if need be. Our site was now ready and we settled in for the long night ahead.

"Hey, Wheat, did you remember to bring the extra battery for the radio?" I asked.

"Shit, I think I forgot it."

"No problem," Jarvis said as he handed Wheatie an extra battery pack. "But don't forget the next time. I won't always be here, good buddy."

Wheatie called in the first sit reps (situation reports) of the evening. We would be calling those in every half-hour all night long. It was our way of letting Capt. White back at the K troop NDP site know that we were all right.

Everything was quiet most of the night. Dan Bock and Pineapple were using Starlight Scopes (night vision devices) to monitor both ends of the footpath. Around 3:00 A.M., we heard some faint noises far off to our left side about one hundred yards beyond the trip flares. All our guys were alerted and everyone nervously rechecked their weapons to make sure the safeties were off and were set to rock and roll.

Every sound was magnified ten times as we strained our ears to pick up the exact location of the enemy. It sounded like a platoon of NVA soldiers were running straight at us! We heard the sound of thick brush being broken down by their boots as they ran closer to our ambush sight.

POP! went the first and furthest trip flare. Through a cloud of thick white smoke it cast a brilliant yellow-red glow on the jungle floor. I strained my eyes trying to see through the bushes to my front. Wheatie radioed to the captain that we'd made contact. POP! went the next flare and we could no longer hold our fire. The world around us lit up like day as M16s and two M60s went off at the same time. Although we still couldn't see the enemy, we continued firing into the darkness. I heard loud squeals all around us and some of the guys detonated their claymores.

All of a sudden, at least thirty wild boars charged through our position yelping like crazy. We were being attacked by a herd of angry wild forty-pound pigs! They tore into our uniforms and gouged us with their sharp tusks.

"Holy shit!" I yelled out firing toward the ground. Guys were running everywhere trying to get out of their way. The large boar were actually on top of some of the guys digging their hoofs into the their backs. I don't know who was more scared, us or the pigs.

Our guns continued firing for the next five minutes until all the pigs had disappeared. I think I'd rather had fought the NVA! Man, those pigs were fast and those tusks were sharp as razors.

With the attack now over, we spent the next two hours until daylight licking our wounds. The body count for that night was twelve pigs KIA and one wounded. That one tasted good the next day.

As the morning sun broke above the treetops, our somewhat embarrassed, torn, and tattered squads slowly and painfully trudged single file back into K troop's NDP. Our fellow ARPs greeted us with loud clapping cheers and the oink-oinks of squealing pigs! Just another day in the 'Nam.

Just One of Those Days

There's nothing like a nice hot sunny day to hit the highway with the top down. The top of a jeep that is! Pops, our platoon sergeant, was driving and Wheatie, my radio operator, was in the back seat. We were on the way to downtown Saigon. It was my job to go into the city and pick up our supply of black berets at a little shop that did a real nice job for us. They even handmade the red and white patch worn on the side where the Allons crest went. I tried to make this trip every two months or so and today was the day.

Driving into the busy city it was hard to believe there was even a war going on. People were busy walking down the streets and all of the little stores were open and trying hard to grab the GIs off the street to come in and buy something. It reminded me of being in any town in the states, except for the strange clothes worn by the Vietnamese people.

We pulled up right in front of the store and left Wheatie in the jeep while Pops and I went in. I picked up two dozen new berets and introduced Pops to the shop owner. I even bought one of those black silk jackets with the gaudy colorful map of Vietnam on the back. If I recall it had something like, "Kill A Commie For Mommie" across the back.

We left the store but waited a few more minutes while Wheatie ran in to buy something. Shortly, I told Pops, "Well, I guess we better be heading back now."

"Hell no, Jack. We're here now! Let me see if my old friend still lives around here."

Pops was the boss so it was all right with me. We even had permission to use the jeep today. Normally the ARPs would just borrow it and hope we didn't get caught! But we still had to be back in base camp by 5:00 P.M. Wheatie came out of the store, jumped in the back seat, and off we went to find the nearest bar to use the phone.

We found one after a few minutes and not only did we use the phone, but since we were in a bar, why not have a beer? Damn, I didn't know they sold beer before 10:00 A.M. Tasted just as good as in the afternoon! Poor Wheatie was stuck in the jeep the whole time. You think I would let our jeep get stolen when we're on official business? One phone call and three beers later we headed down the road again. Wheatie was in back drinking his beer. (I'm mean, but not that mean.)

In about forty minutes, we were driving in the French Quarter of Saigon where the homes were huge and soon we were pulling up in front of one of the bigger ones. Sitting there on at least an acre of neatly trimmed lawn with palm trees surrounding its border, the house reminded me of one of those southern plantation homes. The only thing unusual about this house was the four-foot high wall of sandbags surrounding it. I asked Pops, "What's this guy do, own Vietnam?"

Pops just laughed and said, "No, he works for the government."

We pulled the jeep in the drive way and locked it up. We were met at the door by Pops' friend, his wife, and his seventeen-year-old daughter.

After exchanging pleasantries, we were lead into the living room and in no time were sitting at a large table drinking tea and eating homemade cookies. I really felt out of place sitting in this beautiful house with my dirty uniform, combat boots, and pistol on. I was supposed to be fighting a war, not drinking tea! It was both nice and strange at the same time, but all I wanted to do was get back to the surroundings I was accustomed to and called home.

Before long, we said our goodbyes and headed back to Bien Hoa. When we got there, I presented First Lieutenant Rich, our new platoon leader, with the package of berets. The LT informed me my vacation was over that we'd be going into a bunker complex in the morning. So much for the good life.

In the morning, we loaded up the choppers and headed to just south of Quan-Loi. Pops told us the NVA had been detected around an old complex of bunkers we'd been to only three weeks earlier. I thought the area was too open to hide very many troops. Even Groucho, my point man, said he didn't think the NVA would be hanging around. They were probably spotted just moving through during the night.

Since this area was only single canopy jungle, that meant our choppers could help us in locating any movement on the ground. I yelled over to Jarvis, "I want you to walk backup today and Pineapple to take up the rear."

"Okay Jack, sounds good to me," he said as he handed me a smoke. Jarvis was my closest friend. He had taught me so much in such a short time. Something between us just clicked the first time we met.

I sat by the chopper door and looked out, but wasn't seeing anything. I was reminiscing about my squad. These guys were the best. I never had to tell them anything more than once. I knew each one of their mannerisms and capabilities. I also knew they could handle any problem in a calm and professional manner. I had complete faith in them and hoped they had trust in me, too.

Jarvis tapped me on the shoulder and pointed toward the co-pilot who said, "We're getting ready to go in and the LZ (landing zone) looks pretty cold (no enemy firing)."

"Roger," I answered, taking the safety off my weapon. That was more out of habit than anything else. It didn't take long for the four squads of ARPs to unload and head in the direction of the old bunkers.

The bunkers, which were laid out in the shape of a diamond, were about one hundred yards in diameter and had an opening at each corner. There were eight of these diamonds arranged side by side covering at least a quarter of a mile. The jungle cover was pretty scant with mostly short foliage surrounding the complex.

Each squad was to take one set of bunkers to start with, ours being the third set. My guys were laughing amongst themselves as we approached the first bunker opening.

"What's so funny, guys?" I asked.

"Well, Jack, we all took a vote and decided that today's your day to play tunnel rat." Jarvis said. We always rotated this job within the squad.

"Okay, I'll do it. Ain't no big thing."

I was getting ready when Groucho came up to me, "Let me check out the exit holes before you go in, Jack. I'll be back in a minute," he said and took off.

Even though I was the squad leader, Groucho was the most important man when we were in the bush. He was my point man for the nine months I served with the ARPs and was the best I'd ever seen He could smell the enemy fifty yards away. He could tell you how many and even how long ago they had been in the area.

We learned we had to be careful though while Groucho was guiding us through the jungle. One minute he was on our left side and the next he'd be over to our right. We learned to trust him and not get crazy and fire at just any movement around us. We never walked into an ambush as long as Groucho was on point, though we could have many times. Groucho would outsmart the NVA at their game over and over again. We trusted him with our lives and he never let us down.

After a bit, Groucho returned. "They've been here," he said, "maybe for two nights. Looked like they used these old bunkers as a resting place." I said okay and had Wheatie pass the info on to Lt. Rich. "I don't think they're in this bunker complex, but still be careful, Jack," Groucho warned.

This was my first time at being a tunnel rat and I was excited about it. "How deep is the hole, Wheat?" I asked. "Is it real crowded in there?"

Wheatie just laughed and said, "You're not going to find out until you go in, Sarge!"

"Okay, I get the picture!" I climbed into the small dark entrance, still a little hesitant. Jarvis said, "Go ahead, Jack. You got to pop your cherry some time!" All the guys laughed at Jarvis's joke. I slid into the hole.

I was expecting to fall three maybe four feet, but I must have dropped at least six before hitting the bunker floor with a thud. My eyes now had to adjust to the dark. I had a flashlight, but the beam wasn't very bright. I started scanning my new surroundings anyway. No sooner had I moved my light around this small black chamber when I saw two eyes looking back at me! My heart jumped! Terrified, I dropped the flashlight and pulled the trigger on my CAR 15 rifle. The noise was unbelievable as I emptied my complete thirty-round magazine into the guy. My ears were ringing but I did manage to hear Wheatie call down, "What the hell is going on down there, Jack?"

"I shot one! I shot one!" I hollered back.

Shaking, I was now on my hands and knees trying to find my flashlight in the dark. I finally found it and tried to see through the cloud of dust that now filled the bunker. I didn't see any more NVA around so I hollered back out the hole, "There's only one in here, somebody help me get him out." I was feeling pretty damn proud of myself by this time!

We managed to get me and the dead soldier pulled out. When Lt. Rich came over to check on us, I was sitting on the ground rubbing the dirt out of my eyes. Groucho and all my guys started rolling on the ground laughing uncontrollably.

"What's so damn funny?" I demanded.

Groucho was hard to understand through all his laughing, but he did manage to say, "This Gook's been dead for at least a week! You killed yourself a dead Gook, Jack! It's now a doubly dead Gook!"

My squad sure was having a field day with this! Lt. Rich was even laughing with them. I had to laugh myself. It was a good way to let out the fear that was built up inside me. About this same time we heard M60 fire to our far right side.

Lt. Rich gave the order for the first squad to finish clearing the bunkers and for the rest of the platoon to head for the sound of our machine gun. We found Pineapple 2 firing into the last and furthest bunker complex. He said he had spotted an NVA soldier going into the hole. Within minutes, our men had all the exits covered and we threw two grenades into the first opening. Next, a Chicom (Communist) grenade came flying out at us. We all jumped back and it exploded ten feet from the bunker opening. Lt. Rich gave the word to cease fire and called for our Kit Carson Scout (Vietnamese interpreter). He wanted to take these enemy soldiers alive if we could.

Soon, the first squad returned and reported all the other bunkers were empty. Lt. Rich sent mine and the fourth squad out to check the rest of the area. We split up and cleared a one hundred-yard circle around the other two squads. We saw two NVA soldiers running away, but didn't even have time to fire off a single shot before they were out of sight. My squad set up a secured defensive perimeter.

It only took a few minutes for our interpreter to arrive. I could hear him yelling into the enemy-filled bunker, but I couldn't hear what was being hollered back out. I figured it wasn't very good because another grenade came flying out. I did recognize chu-hau, the Vietnamese word for surrender. I guess they were calling us every dirty name in the book. These guys were really hard core and had a lot of balls, but they weren't coming out!

We couldn't wait forever and finally ended it by throwing in both concussion and frag grenades. It was over in minutes and I watched our men pull out the bodies of the dead NVA soldiers. I said to Jarvis who was the closest to me, "Damn, Jar, that's a girl they're pulling out!"

It was true. There were two male soldiers and two nurses taken out from that bunker. That was the first and only time I'd ever seen a woman NVA soldier. I mean we gave them a chance, they could have surrendered. It really did upset me a little, but those girls really had balls!

That bunker must have been some kind of aid station because we pulled out a lot of medical supplies. We found no other signs of NVA in the area so it was decided we would spread out on line and clear the remaining three thousand yards of jungle on our way back to the newly designated landing zone. It was getting late and the lieutenant said a bomb strike would be put into this area tonight and we'd be back here tomorrow.

We all got on line with about thirty feet between us and started walking toward the LZ. Some parts of the terrain were a lot thicker than others and we got ourselves a little out of line. Some guys were falling behind trying to push their way through large bushes and others had nothing but open trail in front of them.

I found myself right in front of a thicket of bamboo and started working my way through a small open section when I saw the tan uniform of an NVA soldier! He was crouching low to the ground on the other side of the thicket. I tried to raise my weapon but the barrel was caught in between bamboo vines. I knew I was about to die.

I looked into the face of my enemy and saw that he was a only kid, maybe sixteen years old. *I'm about to be killed by a kid* was the only thing that crossed my mind as he jumped up and pointed his AK-47 right at my chest! He was shaking. Our eyes met and he slowly pulled back the trigger of his weapon. The seconds seemed like hours! CLINK! was all I heard. It sounded as loud as an explosion, but I wasn't dead. His weapon had misfired! I tried desperately to get my weapon free. My eyes searched his weapon and I saw there was no magazine inserted. His rifle wasn't even loaded!

I finally freed my own rifle and saw the terror in his eyes. He stood there shaking, shrugging his shoulders as if to say, "Now what?" For some unknown reason, I shrugged my shoulders, too! I mean I could have blown him away but I didn't. My shoulders hadn't even come down yet and the kid was gone! I watched as he ran off and disappeared into the thickest part of the jungle. This whole ordeal had taken less then two minutes.

Now I started to really shake and had to sit down for a moment. Jarvis, who was already twenty yards to my right front shouted back, "Come on, Jack, what's taking you so long?

I slowly stood up and ran over to him. As we walked back to the LZ together I asked him if he saw what had just happened, but he hadn't. I wanted to tell him, but I didn't think he'd believe me. Hell, I didn't believe it myself!

I have often wondered if later that night somewhere in a deep dark bunker, a scared young NVA soldier was telling his comrades. "You wouldn't believe what happened to me today!"

111

The long flight back to base camp seemed commonplace to me as I sat with my back against the pilot's seat. I was thinking about all the strange things that had happened to me today, and trying to make sense out of it all. Jarvis shouted over the roar of the Huey's rotor blades as they beat against the wind, "Happy birthday, Jack."

"What?" I hollered back.

"Happy Birthday! It is your birthday today, isn't it?"

It took me a minute to think about it. "Yeah, it's my birthday all right," I replied with a shit-eating grin. Today I turned twenty-three.

Section Three

Taking A Break

- ♦ Home is Where the Heart Is
- ♦ Little Tidbits
- ♦ Pictures

Home Is Where The Heart Is

August 17, 1969. This was supposed to be one of my happiest days in Vietnam. It was the day I received my out-processing orders to finally leave the 'Nam. In less then ten days I'd be climbing aboard a freedom bird that would take me far away from the jungles of this country I had called home for the past eighteen months.

Even as the orderly room clerk handed me my treasured package of military forms, I had doubts about wanting to leave. I know it sounds crazy, but that's just the way I felt. I even stopped over by the first sergeant's desk. "Hey Top, what if I wanted to extend again, can I still do it?"

He just looked at me like I was nuts. "Haven't you been here long enough? No, it's too late for that, Jack. You should have put in your paperwork two months ago."

"Okay, I was just wondering," I replied as I walked out the orderly room door.

All I had to do now was go to the twenty different places on my out-processing sheet, get them signed off, and I'd be out of here! That was about the same time I slipped on a large rock and landed face first in a muddy pothole. But my papers didn't get wet! I ran off to my hooch before anybody saw me.

I spent the rest of the morning planning the easiest route to get everything done in the fastest manner, but it still took me almost four days to complete all twenty stops. I think I signed more paperwork than when I had first entered the Army. It took me one full day to locate an intrenching tool (shovel). I don't even remember having being issued one, but the supply sergeant said I was. I saw a Vietnamese kid filling sand bags with one so I asked, "Hey, kid, do you want to sell that?" Ten minutes later and thirty dollars poorer I was the proud owner of one worn out intrenching tool.

It took me an hour to clean that shovel and when it was spotless, I presented it to the supply sergeant in return for the final rubberstamp mark on my large stack of papers. As I was leaving the supply room, I saw that same little kid scooting around the corner of the building with the same shovel that I'd just turned in! I often wondered how much money those two had made playing that game over and over again. I didn't really care. I was leaving and that was all that mattered.

I kept getting these mixed feelings though. One minute I wanted to go home and the next I wanted to stay. I'd think about the belated twenty-third birthday party that Ginny had planned for me but even that wouldn't help. How could I leave my men? I had been with them for nine months now. I knew and loved them like brothers! What would happen to them if I wasn't here? Would their new squad leader be a good one? These questions just kept pulling at me. Even the night before when we were at the club and I was going on about how my next cold beer will in the states, I didn't really believe it.

Finally my good friend Jarvis talked to me. "Jack, you have to go home. You've got a family back there. You've served your time. Now go home and forget about this place."

I nodded in agreement and we shared his last soda together. He and my squad were getting ready to leave on another night ambush. I really wanted to go out just one more time, but I'd already turned in my field gear and my weapon, too. All I could do was wave as they headed out.

I went back to my small room to find a cold beer and listen to the radio. After all, I was no longer an active member of the ARPs. I felt like an outcast and felt naked without my rifle. I decided to go to the club and see if anyone I knew was there. I wanted to be around people. I hated this being alone.

I walked into the NCO Club and saw Sgt. Landon from the Air Cavalry Troop sitting at a table right in front of the stage. Even before I reached his table, he hollered out, "Jack, you old son of a gun, what's happening?"

Chuck was also going home so we sat there drinking as we watched a silly floor show. After a few too many beers, we decided that the next morning we'd head for Cam Ranh Bay to party for a day at the in-country R&R (rest and relaxation) Center. Chuck said he knew somebody who could get us in. He was going to bring a friend with him who was also out-processing and the three of us would party one more time together before we all went home. Sounded good to me so we agreed to meet at the chopper pad at ten the next morning.

As I walked back in the direction of my room I was still thinking, *Why couldn't I be like all the other short timers tonight? How come I'm not acting all silly about going home?* Maybe it was because I was a career soldier. I was in for the long haul, a twenty-year man. I knew I'd be back here again if the war didn't end this year. It was all part of being a soldier, it was my job to serve not only in peace time but also in time of war. I now felt more comfortable with my feelings and decided what I really needed was to get a good night's sleep.

First thing in the morning, I went to Chuck's room to make sure he even remembered what we had talked about the night before. I found him sitting up and getting dressed.

"Hey, good buddy, we still going?" I asked. With a slight hangover he answered, "Sounds good to me. Let's go and find Dan then head out to the chopper pad."

It didn't take us long to locate a chopper that was leaving for maintenance at Cam Ranh Bay and soon we were in the air. By four that afternoon, we found ourselves sitting in a small bar called The Soldier's Bar and Grill. We ate, drank, and just plain partied until I couldn't even stand to look at another beer. A group of other 11th Cavalry Troopers joined us and I was really glad when we finally headed out to get some dinner.

We stayed up all night as did the clubs but by 6:00 A.M., I was more than ready to catch a flight back to our base camp. By 7:00 A.M., we found ourselves at the airfield looking for a ride out. A crew chief from a large cargo plane called a Cariboo offered us a ride to Long Binh and we gladly accepted.

The plane was empty except for the three of us so we took a seat right behind the pilot's cabin. As the large propellers started to engage, clouds of black smoke shot out from behind the two large engines. The plane shook and bounced as we rolled onto the main runway. The engines made a tremendous sound, like they were going to explode, and we slowly lifted off the runway and pushed our way into the sky.

Soon all I could see was sandy beaches below as we flew toward the China Sea. The crew chief was talking with the two pilots as we started a slow banking turn to our right. I was just starting to drift off to sleep when all hell broke loose!

The damn plane dropped, plunging toward the cold ocean below. Four large red lights inside the cabin started blinking on and off as an ear-piercing siren went off with a WHA-WHA-WHA noise! I knew I was about to die! I looked across the narrow aisle at my two friends and could see they were as scared as I was. They were both white as ghosts! All I could think was, *Well, Jack, you dumb shit, you really did it this time! You're about to die in the middle of the ocean and nobody even knows you're here!*

I looked up for something to hang on to and found our crew chief bent over laughing! I then looked at the two pilots and saw they too were laughing like crazy. At first I thought maybe I was just seeing things, but then it dawned on me. We'd been had! And a good job of it, too. Those three guys had just managed to scare the shit right out of us Cavalry troopers! At first I was mad, but then I took it for what it really was, one hell of a good joke. Soon we were all able to laugh about it and when they said, "We do that all the time!" We all laughed about it once more. Let me tell you, I was glad when that plane finally landed.

I stopped by the Long Binh post exchange and bought some things to take home and then caught the afternoon convoy back to base camp. The next few days were pretty quiet as I mostly just laid around. I managed to get my bags packed and then spent time on getting my Class A uniform ready. I had to ask the first sergeant how to pin my medals on in the proper order! I even shined my boots for the first time in months! I tried on my khaki's. I must say that I looked rather sharp in my clean, pressed uniform with my ribbons, CIB, shined boots, and black beret.

118

On the morning I was to leave, I went by the orderly room for the last time and picked up my tickets. The first sergeant called me over and presented me with a set of orders. It was my promotion to the rank of staff sergeant (E-6).

"I didn't want to give these to you before because I was afraid you'd only go out and celebrate and get into trouble or something," he said as he shook my hand. I thanked him and hurried off to get new stripes sewn on before I departed on my forty-five minute ride to Tan Son Nhut and my awaiting plane ride home. I still had one thing to do. I had to say goodbye to all my guys just once more.

I found the ARPs all getting ready to leave on their morning mission. This war wasn't going to stop just because I was leaving. I shook all their hands and then gave Jarvis a long hug. We both had tears in our eyes. "Don't worry Jack," he said, "I'll be home in two months."

I didn't really have the time but I followed the platoon down to the chopper pad for one last time anyway. I waved as their choppers lifted off and was soon standing there alone, covered in that damn thick red dust. Water and red dust turns into mud and now my face was covered with it. I didn't care as I slowly walked to my awaiting jeep.

I vowed to never forget those guys, my friends with names like Sam, Bruce, Groucho, Wheatie, Hungerford, Cook, Ike, Lambie-Pie, and Jarvis. But, of course, I did forget many names. Many more than I wanted to.

By the time we finally loaded into the freedom bird, our uniforms were already wrinkled and sweaty. The commercial plane was completely filled and they finally closed the door and we taxied to the main runway. I lucked out and got a window seat and watched all the small white buildings passing by as we made our last turn onto the runway. The jet engines started to rev up. *Well, Charlie, you only get one more shot at me. You better make it good!* That was my last thought before our huge plane rocketed down the short runway and then headed almost straight up into the clouds.

119

As soon as the plane lifted off, the stewardess announced over the intercom, "Up, up and away. Next stop, the world!!" The loud cheers from the inside of that plane could almost be heard back on the ground!

We stopped for fuel in Guam and Hawaii before finally landing at Travis Air Force Base some eighteen hours later. It took us almost two more hours to reach our final destination at the Oakland Army Out-Processing Center. I was there for only six hours, but the guys who were being released from active duty were there even longer. Although we were served a really good steak dinner, a lot of us were too nervous to eat. We just wanted to get back home as fast as we could. Most of our time was mainly spent going from one station to the next getting all of our records checked and rechecked. They paid us, gave us plane tickets if we were going to another post, and in general treated us very nicely.

I took a cab to the San Francisco Airport. I was looking for the war protestors, but didn't find any, only a few long-haired teenagers who gave me dirty looks. I wrote that off as being part of the job. Next stop, home.

The next few weeks were pretty rough for me. I soon found out nobody wanted to talk or listen about Vietnam. It was like they were afraid that I'd go off the deep end or something! Not even Ginny would ask me any questions. It was as if I hadn't even been in the war! But I knew that I had because I was now having the nightmares to prove it. I would toss and turn all night. Sometimes I would yell out, "Incoming!" and roll from the bed looking for a place to hide. This went on for about two months.

I remember one time shortly after I first got home, some kids outside of our house set off a firecracker left over from the Fourth of July. I hit the floor like a shot while Jackie, my young son, laughed. He thought that was the funniest thing in the world. Even Ginny laughed as I slowly crawled out from under the table. In my mind, I was still looking around for my helmet. Over time, things slowly did get better and soon I was reporting to my new job at Ft. Lewis, Washington. I was to be a drill instructor once again.

I found that I hated my new job. All these new young soldiers wanted to know was how many VC I had killed. They didn't understand that it wasn't important how many of the enemy I had killed but rather how many of our guys' lives I had helped protect. That's what war is all about. I didn't like all the spit and polish I had to put up with either.

I lasted at Ft. Lewis for only three months before I signed up for another tour in the 'Nam. I now felt happy again! I couldn't tell Ginny that I had volunteered, so I told her I had gotten orders sending me back. I think maybe she knew, but she never said anything.

Within two weeks, I found myself standing in line at the Oakland Army Center once again. This time it was much smoother processing in because I was now considered a returnee and didn't have to go through the same shit the first-timers had to. No details or any of that junk. I just had to attend two roll calls each day and the rest of the time I was on my own.

I found myself a member in a new group of special soldiers, we were all returning veterans. It was our choice to return. No we weren't trying to become heroes, we were professional soldiers. This was, after all, our job. A job that we took not only seriously but with pride, too. I had found a group of men and a place were I belonged. I felt comfortable at last. There were others who felt like I did! Others who were proud to be called soldiers.

At 2:00 P.M. on January 10, 1970, I once again felt that hot, sticky, humid air hit my face as I walked off the plane in Vietnam. As I looked around at the familiar surroundings I thought to myself, *Welcome back, Jack. Welcome home.*

Little Tidbits

Today these things may seem a little trivial, but at the time they were very important to us. Like any other soldier in any other war, we took a lot of pride in telling everyone what state we were from, how many days that we had left in country, and showing off the names of our vehicles. We worried about the weather, food, R&R, and most of all, the mail from home! This is a collection of little tidbits that I hope you, my readers, might enjoy.

It was almost impossible to remember what day it was or even what month it was for that matter as we didn't do anything by a normal timetable. There were no weekends off or holiday leaves. We worked rain or shine, seven days a week, four weeks a month for the twelve months until it was finally time to go home. On your first day in country, you started with day 365 and counted down until you left on that freedom bird going home! Most conversations started with, "How many days you got left?" Of course with great pride you would reply, "I'm down to 180!" or whatever number of days you had remaining. Everybody did it. Soldiers would have their days written on their camouflaged helmet covers. My remaining number of days was written on an olive drab colored matchbook cover stuck under the elastic band going around my helmet cover. If you only had a month left, the days would be crossed off on a short-timer's calendar which was always carried in your pocket. That was a picture of an almost naked girl with her body separated into thirty sections and you would then color in a section each day during your last month in the 'Nam.

The very first thing any new man in Vietnam did was to get his shiny new helmet cover and write his hometown and state on it. Some wrote it on their flak jacket. I had "California Kid" written on my camouflage cover. The next thing you would do is rub as much dirt on it as you could, then stomp on it to make it look as old as possible! That was so not everybody would know you were an FNG (fucking new guy)! Some of these covers were real works of art and everyone tried to be as original as possible. Everyone in the

'Nam took great pride in showing off their colorful names. You know, there are probably thousands of those old dirty camouflaged helmet covers locked in trunks all around the USA. Just think if they could only jump out and tell us their stories.

Of course, you can't forget about our vehicles either. If it moved on its own or was pulled, it had to have something written or drawn on it. Boy, at times this was a real crazy war! Tanks, ACAVs, trucks, and even jeeps had to have names on them somewhere! While I was in the 11th Armored Cavalry Regiment, my tank was named "Hang Em High" (after the Clint Eastwood movie) and I had a human skull hanging from the main gun tube. I know it sounds a little gross now, but at the time I thought it was pretty cool. While I was in the 1/77th Armored Battalion, I nicknamed my tank the "Double Deuce," which was written on the turret. Most of the ACAVs had names like "Killing Zone," "Sam's Head Hunters," "Cong Eaters" - names which expressed the feelings of the crews that occupied them.

Two of the most sought after things by all soldiers in the 'Nam were mail and hot chow! Lets start off with the mail. One good thing about sending our mail home was the fact that we didn't have to put a stamp on it. We only had to write the word "free" on the upper right hand corner of the envelope. My mail would arrive in stacks of three or four letters at a time. When I first got to 'Nam, I'd get upset if I hadn't gotten mail at least every week. I would be mad as hell and assume that my wife was running around on me. But I soon found myself too busy to worry about such childish things. At first, I wrote almost every day! I would spend hours thinking of how to describe everything about my new surroundings.

I then made the mistake of writing about my first firefight. Ginny answered me back and wanted to know too many things that I couldn't and didn't want to tell her, so I just stopped writing about the bad times and wrote only about the food or the weather instead. Soon I just stopped writing at all. If I sent a letter every three weeks to just let her know I was still alive, I was doing good. I think Ginny and I grew further and further apart because of this fact and my new-found way of life. I felt that my family was now here around me in the 'Nam and not back home. Of course, not everybody was like me, but this was my way of dealing with the mail from home.

Food! The food in Vietnam was not always the greatest. It didn't really taste bad, it just wasn't as good as back home. When our company cooks prepared our meals, we called it hot chow and most of the times it was at least that. We would normally receive one hot meal three or four days a week. It seemed like it was always called pressed or rolled something! Like pressed pork or pressed turkey roll. The roast beef was called roll of roast beef. I'm sure it contained parts of the cow I'd never seen before! We always said that the reason that we ate so much roast beef was because Lady Bird Johnson was selling the Army all of her cows! We nicknamed it LBJ steak and to this day I still don't care for roast beef.

Once in a while when we were in the field, we were served fried chicken. That was by far my favorite meal. I was even known to beg for an extra piece on occasion. On holidays, we would get real turkey with all the trimmings! I mean dressing, peas, even real potatoes, and everything.

C-rations were our main source of food though. We lived on them like the Viet Cong lived on their rice and canned salmon. Whenever we got word that our supply of C's had arrived, I always sent my guys running to the shipment. I loved the C-rats that were produced before 1964 because they contained my favorite items - hot cocoa and cookies! Those special cases of C's were getting harder to find so my guys had to dig through all of them looking at the dates on each box. The other crews must have thought they were nuts!

There was a very small booklet put out by Heinz 57 that showed you one hundred ways to prepare tasty meals out of C-rations. My personal favorite was cooking the ham slices and then spreading the small can of pineapple jam over the top! Sounds good to me right now!

But my all-time favorite treat was our occasional Friday night BBQs when our company was back in our base camp. It was really great and reminded everyone of the BBQs we had back home. The cooks definitely went all out and put on quite a spread. There were baked beans with large strips of bacon on top, potato salad, corn on the cob, big rolls, and all the other fixin's like onions, pickles, and black olives. There were at least three fifty-five gallon drums that had been cut in half and filled with hot red coals. Sitting on top of the screen-covered drums were hot dogs, hamburgers, chicken, and even steaks! You could eat as much as you wanted except for the steaks, that was only one per man. I would listen to conversations about great BBQs back home as everybody was busy chowing down. The aroma from our company area would slowly drift all around the base camp and soon there would be guys from the other units trying to sneak into our chow line! You know those cooks really worked very hard and took great pride in their work.

R&R was a special time for every soldier. Each man was authorized to take one time off for rest and relaxation after completing six months in Vietnam. There were about six different places you could visit, but I went to Hawaii on both of my R&Rs, one for each of my tours in the 'Nam.

My first R&R was a seven-day excursion, but the flight itself was almost sixteen hours each way. We stopped in Guam, which was the halfway point, where I went to a gift store and bought Ginny a real nice pair of pearl earrings. When we arrived in Hawaii, we were met at the airport by a small group of hula girls who presented us with leis. Then we boarded buses that took us to the R&R Center.

It really felt strange being here. I mean only eighteen hours before, I was in a chopper coming back from a mission! When we arrived at the center, we were briefed on how to behave, not get into fights, and don't talk to anyone about our jobs back in the 'Nam. Finally after what seemed like an eternity, they let us off the bus. The R&R sergeant escorted us GIs down the entrance hall of the recreation center where all the wives were lined up on each side of a long hallway.

There must have been a hundred young wives and girlfriends waiting there! Some of the girls just couldn't wait any longer.

126

With tears in their eyes, they ran toward their husbands. Others strained their eyes trying to locate their guys in our large group. Some just stood back. They were actually shaking from nervousness. I saw Ginny, my twenty-two-year-old wife, standing there wearing my favorite pink mini-dress. She was shivering as I gave her a long silent hug. Do you still remember that day, Ginny? I do. I felt very awkward standing there as I was feeling both excited and guilty about the men I had left back in the 'Nam.

Some of the wives didn't have anyone there to meet them. That usually meant that something had happened to their husband or boyfriend and they would just cry on the shoulders of the R&R personnel. I steered Ginny away from them. I saw this same thing on both R&R's. The war didn't go away. Not even now, not even here.

This last story is about the weather and is the hardest one for me to explain. I've lived in almost every state, even spending two years at Fort Lewis, Washington, where it rains all of the time, but I've never seen the type of weather we had in Vietnam! First, I'll start with the unbearable heat. I thought I was used to hot weather. After all, I had lived a large part of my live in southern California, but this was different. It was humid, hot, and sticky. It was like you were wrapped in a wool blanket for 365 days! It took most of us at least a month to get used to the extreme heat. Even when you came back from an R&R, it took at least two weeks before you could work a full day without being exhausted.

There were only two seasons in the 'Nam - the dry season and the wet (monsoon) season. The dust was always there during the dry season. All the track vehicles had to use the outer perimeter road at the base camps and that turned the tore up, potholed road into a giant dust storm. It reminded you of the Dust Bowl days! The vehicles pulverized the dirt into a red powder that was as fine as Johnson's Baby Powder. Everything and everyone within one hundred yards of the perimeter road would be covered with this dust. It got into your hootch, on your food, even showering couldn't get this stuff off!

Then there was the rain. At the start of the monsoon season, solid sheets of rain would sweep across the whole of Vietnam twice a day, everyday, at the same time. You could see this wall of water coming for miles. It wouldn't just rain, but rather it would pour down on you like it was coming out of giant buckets. The guys would actually strip down and with a bar of soap in hand, take a bath during this twenty-minute downpour! And then it would stop and everything would be as dry as a bone. You'd never even have known it rained, except for the double-digit humidity it left behind!

Then the monsoon season would get even worse and it would rain for days at a time, usually at least three or four days, before it would let up for a day or two. Then it would start all over again. Nothing would remain dry. I don't care how well you tried to protect it, everything you owned stayed wet. At least us tankers could use the exhaust from the tank to help dry things off, but the grunts just stayed wet. Of course, all of the roads and trails that had once been covered in a foot of dust now turned into three feet of mud. Everything was covered in that mud - your tanks, your clothes, just about anything you touched.

I hope you felt that hot, humid, sticky feeling like we did and I hope you got soaked along with us. Now multiply that by ten and that's what it was really like!

ARPs lowering flag to half-mass in honor of Frank Saracino

Jim Tanouse, my gunner, on the Double Deuce

Chris Cordova, my driver and good friend, on the Double Deuce

Picture of me in my ARPs uniform

Joe O'neil (Stick) and Chris on the Double Deuce

Me looking cool in my shades

All these ARPs received the Silver Star for valor.
Included are Lambie-Pie, Bruce Stephens, Dan Bock, Ed Cook,
and Lt. Rich

11th ACR Regimental Commander, Col. George S. Patton III
and Air Cav Troop Commander, Maj. (Doc) Bahnsen.
Note the peace symbol

Groucho, the best point man I ever worked with

ARPs and M company tanks on a search and destroy mission

Section Four

One More Time-B Company, 1/77th Armored Battalion, 5th Infantry Division

- ◆ The Cop Gets Canned
- ◆ Our Secret Weapon
- ◆ On Donner, On Blitzen
- ◆ The Road to Nowhere
- ◆ We Just Called Him Chicken
- ◆ The Deuce Takes a Swim
- ◆ Khe-Sanh-My Last Battle
- ◆ Chris Cordova, My Friend
- ◆ Last Flight Out

The Cop Gets Canned

The year was 1970 and the supply of troops from the states had started dropping off. That's why the tanks of my new unit, B company, 1/77th Armored Battalion, 5th Infantry Division, normally only had a three-man crew: the tank commander, loader, and a driver. Having a gunner was a luxury few were afforded, but to my surprise, our company got twelve newbies from out of nowhere and I soon found myself with a full four-man crew.

We got Private Joe O'Neil as our new loader. Since Jim, my present loader, was an E-4 and outranked him, I moved him up to the gunner's position. Joe had been in country for only two weeks and sure looked green around the gills. He said he was from Detroit and had just graduated high school. He had been working as a janitor in one of those auto factories when he got drafted into the Army. Because he was so tall and skinny and used to push a broom, it didn't take me long before I nicknamed him "Stick." Both Jim and Chris liked Joe's new name so it became official and from then on. Stick was all Joe O'Neil was ever called.

I remember the first time Chris and Jim got a hold of him. It was only his second day and he was supposed to be helping with tank repairs. The first thing they did was to call him inside the turret. As Jim was busy cleaning the radios, he told Stick that it was leaking squelch (the sound the radio makes after releasing the transmitter button) and asked him to please go to the communications (commo) track and pick up a couple of cans for Sgt. Stoddard. Excited with his first job and wanting to do it properly, he grabbed his weapon, flack jacket, and steel helmet and rushed off toward the middle of the perimeter. Realizing he didn't know where he was going, he returned a few moments later.

"Where's the commo track, Specialist Tanouse?"

Jim stuck his head out of the turret and pointed to the far side of the perimeter to a lone track with six antennas sticking out its top, "It's that one over there, Stick. And call me Jim, not Specialist

Tanouse. Now hurry up before this squelch leaks all over the place!"

This time Stick took off in a dead run with his helmet bouncing up and down on his head. After a few steps his rifle dropped from his shoulder and landed on the ground. When he went to pick it up, his helmet fell off! He looked so pitiful. He was having a hell of a time, but finally did arrive at the commo track.

Almost breathless, he yelled inside to the two men, "Sgt. Stoddard needs two cans of squelch for Bravo Two-Two. It's leaking out of the radio pretty bad!"

Old Sergeant Murphy just looked at Stick for a long moment as he thought to himself, *Must be another new guy.* He finally said, "Son, I just gave away my last can of that stuff a few minutes ago. You'll have to try and find someone on one of the other tanks to give you some of theirs."

Stick thanked the old sergeant and dashed off to the closest tank. Sgt. Murphy couldn't help but laugh as he thought, *Poor guy just got his cherry popped.* Stick was unmercifully sent from tank to tank. Since everyone had been through it themselves, they gladly played along with the joke.

After about an hour, I realized Stick was missing (I didn't know about the joke yet) and was about to ask my guys where he was when I saw him walking toward the tank looking depressed. He said, "Sgt. Stoddard, I looked everywhere for that damn can of squelch, but I couldn't find any."

It took me a minute to understand what he was talking about, but then it dawned on me. Stick had been had. "Jim, Chris, get over here! What's going on? What did you do to Stick?" They both laughed and confessed their sins.

I looked at Stick and said, "Well, my friend, you have just become a full-fledged member of the Double Deuce," and went on to explain to him that there was no such thing as a can of squelch. From that day on, those three were inseparable and became the best tank crew I ever worked with.

We spent most of the next two weeks around our base camp at Quang Tri never venturing too far. We did go on two night ambushes, but came up empty-handed both times. Finally, our tank company got word we'd be leaving Quang Tri and heading down south toward the Mekong Delta. Stick was very excited about this mission as he hadn't seen much of Vietnam. He bugged me all day with his crazy questions, "How long will it take?" "Will we go through any cities?" "Do we get to drive through Saigon?"

"Yes, Stick. Yes, Stick. Now shut up, Stick," I replied. The kid was driving me crazy!

In order to reach the location of our new mission in the fastest manner, we would be traveling on what was called a Thunder Run. That's where a unit leaves point A and, other than for refueling, doesn't stop until it reaches point B. It could take hours or even days to get to point B, it didn't matter. I figured it would take us around ten hours to get to our destination, fifty miles southeast of Saigon.

Early the next morning, I was already in the motor pool with Chris warming up our tank when I looked up to see Stick running through the mud puddles toward us. He was carrying a large bag of goodies he had bought yesterday and the camera hanging around his neck was wildly bouncing from side to side. I yelled down to him, "Stick, we're not going on a picnic, we're going to war!"

He just gave me a big grin unsure if I was serious or not. I just shook my head as Chris helped him up on the tank. Soon after that, all twenty tanks of B company were heading out the main gate traveling down the muddy twenty miles of secondary road until we reached the hardball (main road) that would take us toward Saigon.

Everything was going great. The Deuce was running fine and Stick was busy taking hundreds of pictures. If it didn't move, Stick took a picture of it! Chris was driving and talking over the intercom with Jim who was resting in the gunner's seat. He would have to drive if Chris got too tired. Stick was jumping up and down on the loader's seat, his body from the waist up was sticking out above the turret. He kept pointing to this and that getting all excited and yelling over the roar of the Deuce, "See that car?" "Look at that water buffalo!" It didn't bother me too much as I knew we were in a pretty safe part of Vietnam, or about as safe as you could be. I didn't want to ruin his fun on this special day, his first mission in a strange new land.

I was starting to do a little daydreaming myself when I felt Stick pushing at my shoulder. He was offering me a Coke and some chips. I took the soda noticing he now had the soft drink, two cans of chips (all food goodies came in cans, not bags), and a can of cookies sitting on top of my turret! I looked down inside to see Jim munching on a handful of chips, too. I was thinking how it was nice that Stick had shared his treats and I could hear Chris talking with a mouthful of food. This was going to be an interesting day for sure.

As we approached the outskirts of Saigon, I told Stick to put all that food stuff away. As he was busy cleaning up his mess, I was thinking that in about two more hours we'd finally be stopping for fuel and I'd be able to stretch my tired legs.

We paused long enough for a military police jeep to get in front of our column so it could escort us through this very large and very populated city. We were informed by radio that the Saigon Police Department would be blocking all intersections on our route and for us to still drive carefully, maintain the proper distance between tanks, and don't run over any civilians!

As we entered the city, Stick was throwing pieces of Double Bubble gum to all the kids standing in the street. When we approached our first intersection, I heard Stick holler, "Look over there, Sarge! There's a general standing on the corner." Stick raised his hand giving this man a very proper hand salute. I yelled back, "No, Stick, that's just a Saigon cop!"

I really need to tell you folks what Stick saw and why he thought it was a general. Close your eyes and picture this: a Vietnamese man standing about five feet tall, wearing shiny black boots, black trousers (neatly creased), a huge military-style black belt with a large gold buckle holding a shiny holster with handcuffs, a three-foot-long black stick and gun, a very clean starched white shirt with large pockets, a shiny gold badge, long gold braid hanging from both shoulders, a pair of pilot-style sunglasses, and a white saucer hat with a shiny black bill! That is what Stick thought was a U.S.

Army general! I was laughing so hard I thought I'd fall off the darn turret. We made it through more than half of the city before our first crisis arrived. Stick was telling me that he had to go to the bathroom! I told him he'd have to wait until we were out of the city and at our first refueling stop. He looked very upset as he dropped back onto the turret floor next to Jim. I looked down and could see that he was bouncing from one foot to the other. About that time, Jim came over the intercom and asked me why couldn't Stick just pee in the empty cookie can? I heard Chris laughing in the back ground and said, "Okay, but be careful!" So here is Stick, peeing into this can with Jim threatening him that if he even spills one drop he would be cleaning up the turret floor for a week.

Soon the deed was done and now Stick was asking what should he do with the can. Before I could answer, Jim told him to throw it out the loader's hatch! I watched in horror as the can of pee turned into a projectile flying high above the turret of the Double Deuce!

I think you know what's coming next, but I got to tell you anyway! That can went almost twenty feet into the air, leveled out and started it's downward journey all without spilling a drop. By now Stick was looking out of the loader's hatch and Jim was yelling for him to move over so that he could watch also. The cookie can was heading straight in the direction of a Saigon cop standing at an intersection! The crew of the tank behind us saw the can flying out our tank and was now cheering at what was about to happen.

Sure enough, the can landed right on its bottom three feet in front of our unsuspecting friend. I watched in total disbelief as the liquid, in what seemed like slow motion, covered him from head to toe with one swift SPLASH! I can still see the surprised and shocked look on his face as he wiped his hands across his dark glasses and smelt them!

Both Stick and Jim knew they were in trouble, but their ass chewing would just have to wait. I was laughing too hard to punish them now.

The guys behind us were roaring as I heard their call come over the radio. "Double Deuce this is Bravo Two-Three, way to go man!"

Next came a call from Bravo Two-One, our platoon leader, "Bravo Two-Two, did you call? Over."

"No, Bravo Two-One, everything is okay back here!" Our new man Stick had just become a legend in his own time! I also think there's one pissed off cop in Saigon. Or should I say, pissed on!

Our Secret Weapon

Don't let anybody tell you the Army doesn't take care of their own. Almost like clockwork, every four weeks we tankers received a large, unmarked sundry box that contained the following:

3 ea. bar soap	1 box tropical candy bars
4 ea. cartons of cigarettes	1 box Chickletts
3 pkg. writing paper	1 box Double Bubble gum
3 ea. pens	1 box jelly candy
4 ea. disposable razors	2 ea. Chrome P-38
1 can shaving cream	1 box book matches

No matter how they arrived, by truck in the dry season or by chopper during the monsoons, it was always an exciting day when the shipment got to us. It was almost like Christmas morning.

As tank commander, I was the one to play Santa and divide up the contents. Otherwise, my guys would fight over everything like a bunch of kids. The crew would sit in a circle on the back deck of our tank and I would slowly opened the sealed outer box and then pull out the three smaller parcels from inside.

First, I picked the box containing the soap, razors, and shaving cream and asked who wanted what. Next came the packs of writing paper and pens. Those normally went to Chris because he was the only one who seemed to write to people. Passing out the smokes was easy, me and Stick were the only ones who smoked and we would split the supply in half. Next came the candy. That wasn't quite so easy and I would let the men fight over it. One of their favorite items was bubble gum. They would each grab large packages of candy and gum and then start to trade and negotiate with each other.

This friendly form of bartering could literally last for hours. But the item no one ever seemed to want were those tropical chocolate bars. In fact, we couldn't give those away, even to the village kids who always wanted some treats from the GIs. This was kind of curious to us since these bars had been created specifically for the hot, humid climate of Vietnam. But whatever they did to them sure made them taste terrible.

Wondering what those sundry kits had to do with the development of a secret weapon? I'll get to that, but first I have to explain a little about the ammunition we carried on our M48A2 tank. Our main source of firepower was the main gun (90mm cannon). It fired a large shell that looked like a rifle bullet except it was almost four feet tall and weighed about thirty pounds. Additionally, there were two mounted machine guns, a 30-caliber coax mounted inside the turret and a 50-caliber one that was mounted on top of the tank and used by the tank commander.

The main gun had four different types of ammunition. One was HE (high explosive) and another was the Sabot round (armor piercing). That ammunition was designed for large cement bunkers or other tanks, both of which were seldom found in South Vietnam. The other two types of ammunition, the ones we used most (accounting for some eighty percent of the main gun rounds), were called cannister rounds.

The newest type of cannister was pointed like a regular bullet and painted olive drab with a slip-ring mounted on it. It could be adjusted for the desired distance to explode from the tank and was filled with literally thousands of inch-long steel, arrow-like darts known as flasets. The other cannister round was the much older version. It was black in color and flat on top, much like a standard shotgun shell except, of course, much larger. This type of round, used by the Army for years, was loaded with small tightly wrapped pellets that would explode from the main gun like a giant blast from a shotgun. It was great for tearing away large chunks of thick jungle.

It was one of those hot lazy days and the second platoon of B company was assigned to road security detail on the main highway between Long Binh and our base camp at Quang Tri. Stick was busy writing a letter home while Chris and Jim were lying on the ground next to the Double Deuce sunbathing and reading comic books. I was sitting on top of the tank commander's seat, pulling guard and trying to read a two-week-old copy of *Stars and Stripes* when I noticed a ¾-ton truck pull off the hardball and head into our small compound. I called down to Chris to put his shirt on since I knew it would only be a matter of minutes before our platoon sergeant, SFC Groves, would be passing out the mail that was surely among the large boxes and other supplies on that truck.

Sure enough, within twenty minutes Groves called on the radio for one man from each tank to pick up their mail and a sundry box for the crew. As the mail and the goodies were being distributed, I spotted a jeep followed by two trucks pull into our position.

"Guys, our ammo has arrived," I informed them. "Let's put that junk away and get busy breaking down those crates. We've got at least two hours of hard work ahead of us." While restocking the ammunition, Stick slipped while bending over a tarp stretched out next to our tank and dropped one of the pellet-filled canisters on its side causing the pressure-sealed top cap to pop off. This wasn't uncommon as I'd seen these caps come loose during the normal day-to-day maneuvering of the tank through the rugged jungle terrain. I was about to chew out my clumsy crew as they were busily trying to recap the dropped round when Chris yelled, "Don't worry, Sarge! We'll take care of it."

I replied in a stern and somewhat irritated tone, "Okay, but you guys better be more careful in the future." It was one thing facing the enemy, but the last thing we needed was to get blown away by our own ammunition!

As far as I knew, the rest of day was uneventful, but I guess my guys couldn't keep what they had done a secret any longer, and later that night decided to confess to me. Unable to find all the spilled pellets from the dropped canister round, they decided to fill the void by packing it full with Double Bubble gum from the recently opened sundry box.

Briefly then, that is how the Double Deuce's secret weapon, the Double Bubble Bullet, came to be. However, it took some time before we had the chance to test our innovation in action.

Our five tanks had been assigned again to a night ambush on the main road, this time just outside our base camp at Quang Tri. We

149

were parked just off the main road next to a section of small hills. This particular section had been getting mined by the Viet Cong almost every night for the past week and it would take hours the next morning to clear it before any vehicles could safely travel on it.

Around 2:00 A.M., a trip flare went off about a hundred yards to our front. Jim, who was pulling guard at the time, gave the command, "Main gun, on the way," as he pulled the trigger and fired the 90mm cannon. I was sleeping on the ready rack inside of the tank when the round went off. I immediately stood on the turret floor and loaded the second round, while yelling, "Up!" as Jim fired once again. We fired one more main gun round before the cease fire command was heard over the tank radio.

It remained quiet for the rest of the night with only the sound of an occasional POP from a parachute flare going off above our small group of tanks. Thank God for those mortar crews who worked through the long jungle nights to help keep us safe.

Early the next morning, our platoon sent out a reconnaissance patrol to search our field of fire from the night before. You wouldn't believe what happened next! When the patrol returned, they reported having found two dead VC soldiers and three blood trails leaving the area. Then, while shaking their heads, they added that one of the dead VC was covered in some strange sticky substance that smelled to them like bubble gum! Our platoon leader just looked at the guys like they were all crazy and said, "Bubble Gum?" Of course, my crew just smiled and we returned to our tank while the reconnaissance patrol was still trying to convince the lieutenant.

It didn't take long before the word somehow got out and other tankers started to make their own "secret weapons." I did know for a fact that even the Old Man's tank had two Double Bubble Bullets onboard. Of course, he never knew it.

On Donner, On Blitzen

It's December and only weeks away from that special morning when Santa arrives. As I watch my two young sons, Chris and Billy, playing on the floor, I'm trying to recall the events that took place on that special day some twenty-eight years ago at our base camp in Quang Tri. That's where the crew of the Double Deuce and I celebrated our first and last Christmas together.

Our tanks were slowly moving onto the outer perimeter road of Quang Tri on the morning of December 25, 1970. All of B company had been in the field for more than two weeks as our commanders remembered what had happened during Tet '68. They wanted to make sure the surrounding area of Quang Tri was not being infiltrated by the North Vietnamese Army. We were planning on continuing our search and destroy missions until after the first of the year, but last night I was informed we would be moving back into base camp the next morning.

The twenty tanks of B company departed our jungle NDP (night defensive perimeter) around 5:00 A.M. and it took us three hours before we finally turned onto the paved road just four miles from the base camp's main gate. The early morning air seemed extra cold and damp and I had Stick, my loader, locate my field jacket for me. I was actually getting cold riding up on top of the Double Deuce as we pushed our way through the thick, prickly jungle twines hanging out over the narrow trails we followed out of the mountains. Jim and Chris were all excited about going back to base camp, if only for a single day. It would be a nice break from our normal routine of the past few weeks and a time for us to relax a little.

Stick had tied down his small eighteen-inch decorated Christmas tree on top of the Double Deuce right behind our main gun tube and I watched the tiny ornaments blow in the wind. We turned onto the hardball road and our long column started picking up speed, throwing large chunks of mud high into the air behind our tanks. It was hard for me to relate the strange surroundings to Christmas. Even though the radio had been playing Christmas music off and on for the past week, it wasn't going to be a white Christmas for us, that was for sure! The weather was still very hot and humid during the day with only the mornings being a little colder giving us a sure sign that it was supposed to be winter.

As we pulled our tanks into the motor pool, I had to remind my guys that we still had two hours of maintenance to pull before we could head for our hooches. They had already begun to act silly as soon as we passed through the main gate into the relative safety of our base camp. As I aligned our tank next to Bravo Two-One, I told Chris to shut her down and get started with the maintenance. I heard the Double Deuce power down and saw Stick and Jim already climbing out through the loader's hatch. My guys knew exactly what had to be done, I never had to tell them. They just went to work and got the job done. I cleaned my 50-caliber machine gun before covering it up for the rest of the day. Like I've said before, we had no days off in the 'Nam and today was no exception.

By 10:00 A.M., we had finished our tasks and we all grabbed our bags of dirty clothes to take to the wash women for cleaning. The local Vietnamese seemed to be moving around working as normal. I don't know if they celebrated Christmas or not. As I climbed down from the Deuce, I said to it, "Merry Christmas, girl," and headed for my rarely occupied hooch. We didn't get to spend much time in our base camp, maybe twenty days out of the whole year.

I hollered to my crew who were now almost a hundred yards in front of me approaching our company area, "You guys stay out of trouble. I'll see you at 3:00 P.M. for dinner!" They all yelled back, "Okay, Jack, we'll see you then," and ran off toward their hooch.

I spent the rest of the afternoon just talking and joking around with the other NCOs. We drank a few cold beers, played some cards, and waited for that big Christmas meal that would be served in just a short while. The songs of the season were being played on the radio in the background and I couldn't help but think of how depressed I was getting. It seemed like the more I heard that Christmas music, the more homesick I got. That was the last thing I wanted to feel. I knew tomorrow would find me still in Vietnam and back into the bush as if today had never even happened.

Around 2:00 P.M., Jim stuck his head inside my hooch and asked if he could talk to me outside. I said sure and wondered what kind of trouble he had gotten himself into now. I walked outside and found Jim, Stick, and Chris all standing there. Jim then handed me a small wrapped gift and said, "This is from all of us. Merry Christmas, Sarge."

I was feeling a little guilty about not getting them anything as I opened the package. It was a Zippo lighter and it had some writing on it. It read: *To The Deuce* and was signed *Jim, Chris, and Stick.* Then below their names it read, *The Crew Of Double Deuce, 1970.* Tears came to my eyes and I thanked them for their special gift. They just nodded, looking a little embarrassed and said, "It's no big thing, Deuce." Deuce was my nickname because I was the commander of Bravo Two-Two. It was really special to me when they called me that. I really did, and still do, love each one of those three great guys. We were even closer than brothers. We were brothers of the 'Nam. I went back into my hooch and proudly showed all the guys my present.

At 3:00 P.M., I joined the long line of fellow troopers outside our mess hall. Soon the doors opened and the aroma of freshly cooked turkeys filled the air around us. We entered a room that had been transformed into Christmas itself! The walls were decorated with banners proclaiming the Christmas season and in the corner was a brightly decorated tree. Where that came from, I'll never know. It reminded me of the other five Christmases I had spent in the Army. I could even remember seeing much of the same type decorations in my Dad's mess halls many years before when I was a small boy and our family attended Christmas dinner with the men of my Dad's outfit.

The tables were all covered with white tablecloths and plates full of nuts, candy, and a fruitcake had been placed in the center of each one. The food looked almost too good to eat as we slowly moved toward the chow line. I had made sure my crew was in line in front of me. Even on this special day, I was still looking out for my guys. The Chaplain and all of our officers were standing in the front of the line shaking the hands of their troopers. It was really quite moving. A lot of the younger soldiers were amazed at the effort our cooks had gone to make this a day to remember.

As I sat down to enjoy this fantastic meal, I couldn't help but think of all the other men who wouldn't be eating this kind of food today. They'd be eating C-rations and stuck far away from any Christmas trees or decorations. I thought to myself, *We're the lucky ones,* and I silently raised my glass of Kool-Aid in a toast. That was the best I could do.

A few of the men brought in a small record player and started singing Christmas carols next to our tree. I must admit, I did enjoy watching my guys having such a good time, much the same way I enjoy watching my kids today.

Before I left the mess hall, I reminded Chris about the special church services tonight at 7:00 P.M. I spent the rest of my day just lying around as I had eaten way too much of that fresh turkey. I couldn't even sit up to play some cards!

Our wakeup call came too early for me the next morning, but I soon found myself loading up our tank with my freshly cleaned clothes and getting ready to head back out into the boonies. It wasn't very long before the tanks of B company were cranking up and clouds of black smoke filled the motor pool. The ol' Double Deuce started to move out and I called down to Chris, "On Donner, on Blitzen." I saw our little Christmas tree lying on top of the motor pool trash can. *Well, I guess that means Christmas is officially over for another year.* Little did I know it would be the last Christmas for one member of my crew.

As soon as our tank company got to our prearranged destination, we broke into platoons and continued driving for about another hour until we, the second platoon, found ourselves high on the side of the grass-covered mountain that was to be our home for the next week. Trucks brought bulldozers to the foot of the mountain. After they were unloaded, the bulldozers slowly drove up the steep side. They spent almost one full day cutting us a series of tank-firing positions. Even with the huge mounds of fresh dirt piled in front of our tanks, we had a great view of the jungle and rice paddies below. If I looked through my binoculars, I could just barely see our base camp back at Quang Tri, some thirty miles away.

During the day, we would go on patrols, taking our tanks out a little further each time. The senior NCOs and officers had already begun to warn us that on New Year's Eve there would be no outbursts or firing of weapons at midnight. If they told us once, they told us a hundred times! Of course we all counted down the days until it was December 31. Nobody made a big deal of it and around 8:00 P.M., we started our guard duties as normal. It was just like any other night, except for the little more than average whispers heard around the NDP.

It was now five minutes to midnight and I could see all the crews of the second platoon were sitting on top of their turrets. We listened to our muffled transistor radios as the countdown began. At the very same instant that the voice on the radio cried out, "Happy New Year, Vietnam," the whole sky above our small isolated perimeter lit up as pop-up flares, regular flares, smoke grenades, and rifles went off! It was completely crazy as everyone was yelling and running around firing their M16s. Those were loaded with nothing but tracer ammo and sent a solid line of red-colored bullets flying high into the air. All the guys were cheering it up as we all knew this was the year we'd be going home. Well, so much for the warnings. Boys will be boys you know.

I looked out into the valley below us. It was an unbelievable sight. It looked like the whole country was lit up! You could see where every one of the small fire bases were located in a thirty-mile radius by the green and red flares going off high above their perimeters. Even our own base camp looked like it was fighting World War III! The firing must have gone on for at least fifteen minutes and you know we all got our butts chewed real good the next morning. But you know what? I even saw our platoon leader standing side-by-side with our platoon sergeant firing off red flares from the inside of our perimeter! Men will also be men!

Well, that was what it was like for me at Christmas and New Years in Vietnam. This Christmas, just like the past twenty-eight years, I'll stand up at the dinner table and give my normal toast. It's normal to me, but isn't completely understood by my friends or relatives. I don't think they really understand who the "us" is, but I really don't care. I just stand up and say, "Here's to those who wish us well and those who don't can go to hell!"

The Road to Nowhere

It was pouring down rain as the Double Deuce began moving slowly out of the motor pool. I felt sorry for Stick as he took his position on the ground, ten feet in front of us. He had the unpleasant task of ground-guiding our tank around the outer perimeter of Quang Tri, our base camp. As he stood in the rain, I could see the red mud was over the tops of his boots. We were given the command to move out and since we were the lead tank, I yelled down to Stick to get moving.

As he headed for the perimeter road, you could see that he was having problems as his feet were already getting stuck in the mud that would only be getting deeper. It was only a quarter of a mile to the front gate of Camp Red Devil, but it would take us forty-five minutes to get there. This narrow road was used only by tracked vehicles and in a short period of time it had turned it into a series of large ruts and giant potholes that were now filled from the daily downpour of monsoon rain.

It was slow going as our fifty-ton tanks dug into the soft mud and climbed up a small knoll only to slide down the other side. By the time the Double Deuce finally reached the front gate, poor Stick was covered with mud from his waist down. He tried to climb up the front slope of our tank, but it took him three tries before he made it up onto the front fender. Of course, it didn't help that Chris had been laughing at him from the driver's compartment the whole time.

I felt a strange sense of urgency about this particular mission. One reason was that it hadn't been preplanned and the second was the command wouldn't tell us where we were going or how long we'd be gone. For the next full day, I took my directions from our platoon sergeant, Sergeant First Class Groves. All he would say was things like, "Turn left at the fork, etc." One thing I did know was by the end of that first day, we were no longer in South Vietnam! I'd been around long enough and had worked in almost all of our regular areas and this was not one of them.

As our tank platoon descended into the wide open and rain-soaked green valley before us, the word to pull over was given. I could see a bladder (a large rubber container) of fuel lying just off to the side of the grass covered trail we were traveling. Upon further inspection I could also see five Mermite containers which held the evening chow for the platoon. But that would have to wait until after the refueling and maintenance of the tanks was completed.

The rains had finally stopped. So after chow, my crew dried out their sleeping gear, sleeping bags, and poncho liners by hanging them over the back of our tank so the hot exhaust could blow through them. This would only take minutes to accomplish and soon the five tanks of B company were busy setting up the night defensive position in this strange new area.

It was an uneventful night and as the sun was starting to break over the top of the jungle, our small group was already moving through the wet elephant grass climbing our way out of the valley. On the second day, we traveled deeper into this virgin territory. The mountains were getting a lot steeper and it was getting tougher to fight our way up the soft, muddy slopes. It took us all day to cross two of the thick jungle-covered ridge lines before we finally came to a halt high on the peak of the third one. It was 3:00 P.M. and my crew and I were totally exhausted! Pushing your way through the jungle wasn't easy. It was an all-day fight trying not to get knocked off the tank by those damn thick branches, vines, poisonous snakes, and God only knows what else! However, we were all excited because tonight was to be the night that we'd finally find out where we were going!

Soon I could hear the Chinook helicopter overhead as it lowered another fuel bladder into the middle of our tight perimeter. SFC Groves gathered all of the crews together and told us that by tomorrow morning we'd be at our final destination, which was about five miles from here. He said we could have made it today if the terrain had been better and we weren't all so tired.

Our mission was to proceed to hill 889, wherever that was, and bring out two large, towed howitzer artillery guns that had been providing protective fire for our bombers working in the north. There were also supposed to be two platoons of Special Forces Rangers and a group of Montagnards. The Montagnards would remain behind since their home village was only a short distance away.

I was excited by this news! I'd always wanted to meet a real Green Beret. Up until now, I'd only seen them in the movies and once I had passed one while walking through the San Francisco Airport. These guys were the best of the best as far as I was concerned!

So far this operation had gone pretty smoothly and as I fell asleep that night, I had a funny feeling that it wasn't going to stay that way for long.

The twice-a-day rains had started to take their toll on our tanks. Early the next morning, we were now facing our next obstacle - a very large and steep mountain. Our first tank barely managed to make it to the first crest line. The second tank only made it half as far before it started its uncontrollable slide backwards, almost hitting the third tank in line. All the gunners and loaders had to gather up the heavy tow cables from each track, hook them together, and then hook them to the tank that did make it so it could pull the rest of tanks up the mountain. It took us hours to get up the steep, muddy slopes pulling one tank at a time, digging ourselves deeper and deeper into the giant hole we were creating. This was one of those times that made being in the infantry look pretty good!

By late morning, we were finally looking into the barrels of the two artillery pieces. We spent the rest of the day hooking up the two forty-ton guns to the tow hooks on the rear of Bravo Two-Three and Bravo Two-four. We also tried to clean the built-up mud from the tank's suspension system but as our luck would have it, the heavy afternoon rains started falling.

The Montagnards departed at daybreak as the dark black smoke from our engines slowly filtered its way above the jungle floor. Hopefully, the return trip would be much faster since we had left a smashed jungle trail behind us. Normally, we'd never take the same trail twice but since we made no enemy contact on the way up, I was sure we'd follow the same one back. Bravo Two-One and Two-Five took the lead followed by the two tanks that were towing our newly acquired guns. The Double Deuce would be bringing up the rear. Each tank also carried five of the Rangers on its back deck.

Even though we weren't too high up, we were driving on an extremely narrow trail and our rubber tracks pads were barely hanging on to the side of this mountain. For the first hour, everything was going fine. I was even telling Chris over the intercom how easy this was. Boy, did I eat those words in a hurry as we came to the first of many steep, downhill slopes.

The first two tanks went down the fifty-foot embankment just fine, but the third tank that was towing one of the guns started to have problems right away. Because of the combined weight of over ninety tons, it immediately started to slide off the mountainside! The driver tried to follow the two deep ruts in front of him, but the tank now had a mind of its own. As it slid, it started to hit the trees closest to it. To say this was a serious situation would be an understatement. Not only could the tank just plain slide off the mountain, but the trees it was hitting could snap in half and fall on top of the tank injuring or killing the crew. Or while the tank was sliding, it could flip over the mud that it was building up.

By the time Bravo Two-Three had reached the bottom, six very large trees had been knocked off the mountainside and two of the Green Berets had fallen off. Thank God they didn't get hurt. We decided for safety reasons to relocate them to the non-towing tanks.

Next came Bravo Two-Four. It also was in trouble from the get go! The driver tried to go around the damaged area caused by Bravo Two-Three, but he panicked and hit the brakes causing the howitzer to jackknife. Now in a V shape, the tank and howitzer both slid the rest of the way down the mountainside, tearing away anything in their path including trees, bushes, and giant piles of soft dirt. They were lucky they didn't actually flip! Bravo Two-Four had managed to throw off not one, but both of its tracks. It would take all of us working together over two hours to dig out and untangle this mess.

We ended up using my tank as the braking system for the howitzers by hooking two tow cables between us and using my brakes to help slow us down the steep grades. It was almost midnight before we reached our NDP sight in the green valley where we had stayed earlier on our trip.

I was really glad that the hardest part of our mission was over. The rest of the roads were in much better shape and posed no problems for us. Once again, we waited for our fuel and, hopefully, some hot chow to arrive. The platoon sergeant from the Rangers asked if we had made any contact with the enemy and when I said we hadn't, he told me that we had been very lucky. SSG Burns told me the reason they had to relocate their guns was because the VC had been shelling them with mortars for the past few nights. Let me tell you, I was really alert that night or what was left of it. But once again, it was very quiet.

We took things a little slower in the morning. We spent extra time working on our tanks but when I fired up the Double Deuce, a large cloud of white smoke appeared and wouldn't go away. Soon the tank was covered in smoke. I had Chris try to move it forward, but it just stood there. I'd been a tanker long enough to know a blown engine when I saw one! What else could go wrong on this mission?

Two hours later, after receiving word form the rear, it was decided the whole platoon would stay with us until the M88 (track recovery vehicle) arrived to help install a new engine that was already being sent by Chinook from our base camp.

By two in the afternoon, the M88 had arrived. My crew and two tank mechanics who had flown in with the engine were busy unhooking the damaged one. SFC Groves took the rest of the platoon, marked were they would be on my map, told me to get this job done ASAP and meet them tomorrow afternoon. We really had our work cut out for us, but at least they had left five of the Rangers to help provide security while we worked.

We worked through the night and by nine the next morning we watched the Chinook carry our old engine over the treetops and out of sight. The Double Deuce was now sounding strong! The best I

161

ever heard her. By now Jim, Chris, Stick, and I were both really dirty and tired. We had been working for almost twenty-four hours straight and as we left this peaceful valley, I couldn't help but think how this beautiful place had caused us so much trouble.

I took the lead while the M88 with its three-man crew followed behind me. I had one ranger sitting on each front fender, two on the back deck, and the platoon sergeant was sitting right behind me. Once again I checked to ensure everybody was okay before we moved out of the valley and into the awaiting jungle ahead.

Soon we were in the thick unforgiving jungle following the trails left by our platoon the day before. As we started to take the fork to the left and through the clearing, all hell broke loose! First I heard the sounds of three AK47s opening up on us. Then I could see the green tracers flying over my head and bouncing off the turret of the Deuce! I cranked back the charging handle of my 50-caliber machine gun while at the same time being concerned about the two rangers on my front fenders. I yelled to them to get out of the way and then opened fire.

The other three Green Berets had already started to lay down a barrage of bullets. At the same time I could hear the 50-caliber on the M88 to my rear kick in with its own POP-POP-POP! Once my front fenders were clear of soldiers, I told Chris to kick it in the ass so we could get to the other side of the clearing. I gave the command, "Main gun!" and as I heard Stick say, "Up," Jim pulled the trigger of the 90mm cannon, spraying the area with a canister round containing thousands of small pellets. He repeated this action two more times before the M88 and us finally cleared the kill zone.

The Rangers were still firing their weapons. I yelled, "Cease fire," and took a visual count of our isolated small group. I was still shaking from what had just taken place. That was one hell of a scary five minutes!

Three hours later, our safe but tired small group finally met up with the rest of the second platoon. As the five Green Berets were loading into Hueys, the crew of the Double Deuce waved good-bye.

We Just Called Him Chicken

A lot of soldiers in Vietnam had pets. Some guys had snakes, some had monkeys, and a few had small dogs. But not the crew of the Double Deuce, we had a chicken! That's right, a chicken! It all happened one day as the second platoon of B company was on a search and destroy operation just east of Quang Tri, our base camp. Our five tanks were driving through a small hamlet of about a dozen bamboo hooches when we had to stop so the platoon sergeant could check our location on the map. Stick, my loader, automatically climbed out from the loader's hatch and with a box of candy in his hand headed for the front fender of the tank. Chris had already gotten out of the driver's compartment and was waiting for Stick. They then proceeded to pass out the candy to the little kids who had gathered around.

I was always a little uneasy about letting the kids get too close to our tank. I had never seen it, but had heard stories about kids throwing grenades into parked tanks. I yelled down to my guys, "All right, you two, don't let those kids get too close and be ready to move out at any time. We're not going to be here very long!"

"Okay, Sarge, this will only take us a minute." they answered back.

They finished passing out all the candy to the ten or so youngsters who were jumping around the Double Deuce. I watched as Stick made sure a little girl way in the back got a piece of bubble gum. Jim, my gunner, was now sticking his head out of the loader's hatch thinking about getting out, too.

"Okay, guys, this isn't a rest stop. We'll only be here a minute," I said as an old man approached our tank. He wanted to sell us a chicken that he was carrying in a handmade straw basket. I motioned for him to leave and hollered out, "De de mou! De de mou!" That means leave in Vietnamese. About that time, Jim said, "Let's buy the chicken, Sarge!"

"What are we going to do with a chicken?" I inquired.

"We're going to cook him for dinner!" my whole crew said in unison.

"Who in the hell knows how to skin a chicken around here?"

"I do!" replied Chris. "He'll taste good when I get done with him!"

I started to say no, but soon they were all begging me so I gave in and said, "Okay, but you'll have to buy him. And I don't want to see any chicken shit on my tank!"

A deal was struck just before we had to depart the hamlet and for twenty bucks we were the proud owners of a live chicken! We carried that chicken-in-a-basket around with us for the rest of the day until we finally stopped for the night. After my guys had set up our NDP (night defensive perimeter), they decided to take the chicken out of the basket. I couldn't believe what that bird looked like! I know I'm only a city kid, but even I knew that a chicken was supposed to have some meat on it! This poor thing was all skin and bones. Even Chris, our resident expert, said it was the skinniest chicken he'd ever seen!

We all had a good laugh and decided we should turn this poor bird loose, but Chris said we should at least feed him first. Jim pulled out a can of those C-ration crackers, you know the ones that are about three inches in diameter until you add water and then they grow to the size of an eight-inch pancake! The guys fed the chicken crackers and water until he was full then they put him on the ground next to our tank. It just sat there flapping its wings for a while and then ran off under the tank.

It was now getting dark, so we all took our normal sleeping positions for the long night ahead. Mine was inside of the tank. I would put my air mattress on top of the 90mm ammunition ready rack. That way I'd be close to the radio and have quick access to the weapons in case we had to use them during the night. (I don't think I ever really slept during those two years in the 'Nam.) Stick would always sleep in the bussel rack just behind the man pulling guard. Chris and Jim would roll out their sleeping bags under the rear of our tank. We rotated the guard duty in three-hour shifts with me always pulling the last shift. That way, I'd know if somebody had fallen asleep and screwed up the rotation.

At 5:00 A.M., the chicken went off! "God dammit!" I hollered out as I had just spilled hot cocoa all over my front. That chicken had scared me half to death! I could hear Stick laughing at me from inside his sleeping bag. "Shut up, Stick," I whispered back at him half-heartedly.

An hour later my, crew started getting up to enjoy another great new day in the 'Nam. Chris went to check the engine oil levels and Jim and Stick went out to fold up our barbed wire and bring in our trip flares and claymores. I stayed busy putting away the makeshift cover that had been over the tank commander's hatch during the night.

Soon everything was done and it was time for my morning tank commander's meeting. I told Jim to pull guard until I got back and then started to walk away.

"What do we do if the chicken comes back?" asked Chris.

"I don't think we have to worry about that. He's long gone by now," I said as I headed for SFC Groves's tank.

When I got back, I found Chris and Stick feeding the chicken on the back deck of the tank.

"What's going on guys?" I yelled up at them.

"He came back. Can we keep him?" begged Stick.

"I don't care. I really don't have time for this now. We have to move out in ten minutes." I pointed to Chris to get in the driver's hatch.

The chicken then jumped off the tank and I thought, *That's one less thing to worry about.* The old Double Deuce started up with a roar and a cloud of black smoke shot out from her exhaust as we started moving forward. I sat and watched that damn chicken jump up onto the rolling track, ride it up to the fender, and then hop onto the tank! It acted like it was no big thing as it walked and then flew up to the turret between Stick and me and just sat there! Now the crew of the Double Deuce consisted of four men and one chicken.

That bird did some real crazy things like walk all the way down the length of main gun tube and sit at the very end flapping his

165

wings as we drove down the road. This must have looked absolutely bizarre to anyone standing along the road. I remember once while we were in a convoy heading to Saigon, we passed our company commander standing by a jeep. I rendered a snappy hand salute as chicken flapped his wings on the end of the tube. Our CO just stood there shaking his head.

Chicken loved to jump off and on the tank while it was moving and enjoyed riding next to Stick. I think that was because Stick always had something to eat. That darn bird would even eat canned chicken!

The guys started calling him Chicken and soon he would come if you called his name. He was great at pulling guard, too. Nobody could get closer than fifty yards before Chicken would sound off. But I never could stop him from clucking at five every morning. All the other tank crews liked our pet, but we did have to put up with being called the "Chicken Guys" from time to time!

Three months later while we were in base camp and I was away at a meeting, it finally came to an end for our pet. The guys were busy changing a large road wheel on the tank while Chicken was sleeping in his favorite spot under the tank. One of the heavy tools slipped and hit him right in the head. As I was going back into the motor pool, I saw him lying on top of the large trash can next to our tank. Boy was I pissed! I ran over to my crew and demanded to know had happened to our pet. The guys told me and Stick even had tears in his eyes as he explained. It was a sad day for the crew of the Double Deuce. It was just like losing a friend, but we had a lot of good times after that just sitting around and laughing about that damn chicken.

The Deuce Takes a Swim

B company was on another Thunder Run. A Thunder Run, as I explained earlier, is where you leave point A and don't stop until you reach point B. We were going down south toward Dak To to support a multi-unit operation and our tanks had to cross a very large mountain range in order to get there.

That was never easy for the twenty tanks that made up a tank company, especially in the middle of the monsoon season. Sometimes it would be raining for days and the tanks would actually slide right off the muddy trails and down the sides of the mountain. And climbing up the steep hills wasn't any easier. If you were lucky, the first couple of tanks would make it just fine, but the tanks behind them would usually get stuck in the deep ruts. We would then have to stop our column and spend hours pulling all the remaining tanks up the steep grades with tow cables. Not only did the tanks get covered in mud, but the crews did, too.

We'd been driving on the mountain trails (they weren't wide enough to be called roads) for about three hours when I was forced to stop. In front of us sat a massive tree that had fallen across our path. It was at least fourteen feet in diameter and eighty feet long. There was no way around it. It was so big that even sitting high up on the tank I couldn't see over it. Since I was in the lead, I immediately looked around for signs of a possible ambush. My next step was to inform our platoon sergeant, Sergeant First Class Groves, who was two tanks behind me. It was quickly decided we would have to blow up the tree in hopes that the small explosion would cause it to slide down the mountain and off the trail.

All we had were Bangalore Torpedoes, so two of my crew members, Jim, and Stick, helped me unload five of them from our storage boxes. Using detonation cord, we wrapped the four-foot-long interconnecting tubes filled with high explosives around the huge tree trunk. This was the first time we had ever tried doing anything like this and Stick kept saying, "I think we need more explosives, Sarge. That's one hell of a big tree."

167

After wrapping all the explosives around the tree, I told everybody in sight to take cover behind their tanks. Groves reached for his hand mike and informed the column over the radio that we were about the blow the tree. Then we backed up the Deuce as far away as we could, maybe fifty feet. I had my driver, Chris, close his steel hatch while Jim and I proceeded to a safe hiding place behind our tank. Stick was busy getting himself in the tank. He said he didn't want to be outside but in the tank where it was safe.

With a nod from Groves I yelled, "Fire in the hole!" Since I had never blown anything up before, I didn't know what to expect. So with hesitation, I closed my eyes and squeezed the handle of the detonating device.

BANG! The whole damn tree just disappeared taking half the mountain with it! The ground shook and our tank moved sideways, too. The concussion threw Jim to the ground and I was clinging to the back of the tank with both hands. Through a large cloud of smoke and dirt, I saw huge splinters hurling over my head and flying back as far as 200 feet to the middle of our tank column.

After the chunks of wood stopped flying, I stuck my head around the tank to see what had happened. When I saw half the mountain missing and a huge hole in the ground where the tree used to be, my first thought was, *Holy fuck, what the hell did I do?* I'm sure as hell no demolitions man.

I picked Jim up from the ground and said, "I guess we overdid it, what do you think?" All Jim could do was stand there wiping the dirt from his eyes and shake his head in disbelief. It took at least ten minutes for all the smoke and dust to finally clear. There wasn't a piece of tree bigger than a twig to be seen anywhere!

Since we were on an important mission, we didn't have time to sit and really take in what we just did. We quickly navigated our way around the hole and were on the move again. My crew and I did feel pretty damn proud of ourselves though. Of course, that was the last time anybody ever asked us to blow anything up.

Hours later, our long column of tanks finally started descending from the bug-infested jungle trails we'd been on all day. A call came over the radio from SFC Groves for me to pull over because his tank had just thrown a track and he was broken down in the middle of the road. It was not uncommon to throw a track while maneuvering around sharp turns and twisting trails, especially if the crew had failed to take the time to properly adjust the tension.

I felt sorry for his crew when I heard what their problem was. It was a lot of work getting that track back on. Sometimes you could walk it back on by moving your tank forward very slowly and using a large pry bar called a tanker bar to force the track back into place. Other times, however, all you could do was break the track in half, run it over the sprocket, and then put it back together again using track jacks. This could take at least an hour to accomplish and was very dangerous work.

I saw a small cliff just ahead of the Deuce and decided to have Chris back onto it. This would give us a great field of view so that we could provide protective cover for our column that was now stalled on the side of the mountain. For all we knew, this area could be hostile. You learned real fast in the 'Nam it was better to assume the enemy was watching your every move because most of the time they were.

As I watched one of the platoon sergeants' men walking toward us, I knew their attempt to walk the track back on had failed. Sure enough, Larry wanted to borrow our two track jacks so I reluctantly gave him our tool bag while Chris was busy lecturing him on the proper procedures for the care and maintenance of their own tools. Chris took a lot of pride in the upkeep and maintenance of our equipment and did not like loaning it out to anyone. Good working tools were often as important as our weapons.

While all this was going on, our platoon sergeant received a message from our company commander saying our mission had just been changed. We were now to proceed to a new destination as soon as possible. Our assistance was urgently needed as units of the 1/61st Infantry Battalion were under heavy attack thirty miles away. See, I told you that the enemy was always around! The crew of Bravo Two-Four hurried about the task of repairing their tank and I informed my guys of the new situation. Within twenty minutes, B company was on the move once again.

169

SFC Groves was going to assume the lead position now and signaled me to fall in behind our last tank, Bravo Two-Five. As the four tanks of the second platoon rolled by me, the Double Deuce started to tremble. I now realized just how unstable this cliff was that I was sitting on! As the Deuce was rocking, I had to be sure Chris understood my every command. We weren't playing any games now. One false move and we'd slide off the mountain. Slowly we moved forward until I determined we were on solid ground. Then I told Chris to neutral steer (pivot) the tank to the left and as we started our turn, I heard a loud POP! Our right track had snapped off over the top of the sprocket that once guided and kept it in place. "Oh, shit!" was the only thing I could think of saying at a time like this. I really felt like a jerk now. My crew took a lot of pride in the fact that we hardly ever threw a track! It was a way of showing the other tankers how good you were. We didn't look too good now.

I yelled at Chris to stop and we tried to back up as much as we could so the column could move around us. I knew this would damage our track even more, but I had no choice in the matter. I radioed Bravo Two-Four and Groves swore and told me to hurry up and get my tank fixed ASAP. I do remember my ears were burning after that conversation.

Soon, the other tanks were out of sight and my crew and I started checking out the damage. I stood on the ground looking at my completely destroyed track and again all I could say was, "Oh, shit!" About that time, Chris walked up to me. "Sarge, Bravo Two-Four never brought back our tool bag."

I could see the fear on his face when I slammed my helmet to the ground. I had to walk away for a few minutes to cool off. I knew I had to call the platoon sergeant again. Now I really felt like a dummy and knew I'd be getting my butt chewed for sure. Oh, what the hell. What are they going to do, send me to Vietnam? There was no place worse than this. It was turning into a real shitty day!

I made the call, but could hardly hear SFC Groves. He told me to just stay put (like I could go anywhere) and he would try to get back to me later. I started getting the guys organized and put Jim in the tank commander's position while I checked out the surrounding area. We were alone on the side of a mountain and I didn't like it here. I got a strange feeling in the pit of my stomach.

It was getting dark before we finally heard an unknown call sign trying to reach us on the radio. I answered and was told to go to their frequency. I was informed a bridge tank would be at our location early in the morning to help us out. Now the night, the mountain, and the enemy would be all ours. I was really nervous about this. Even more than if I were in a firefight because we had no support of any kind. The enemy could have easily snuck up on us from three sides - the mountain above us or the bends in the road on either side of us.

We set out everything we had that night! We put out barbed wire, twenty feet on both sides of the tank, claymore mines, and eight trip flares. We put two of the flares on the mountainside which was directly above our turret because that was the area I was most concerned about. That was our weakest point. I don't think any of us got much sleep that night. In fact, I had us pulling two-man guard duty, that's how worried I was.

Just before daybreak, we heard a tank coming to our rescue. It had been a long and much to our relief, uneventful night. But now we had to get ready to leave. I was still glad we took the extra precautions though.

Soon I saw a tank come into view. It was the bridge tank all right, but it didn't have a bridge on it. I found out later they had left it in position about twenty miles away where it was used by our tanks the day before. And guess what? They had no brakes on their track and were forced to back up the mountain to our location! I had a feeling today was going to be just as bad as yesterday. The two men on the bridge tank were yelling for Jim to throw a worn-out section of track under the front of their tank so when they shut it down it wouldn't roll back down the mountain.

I just shook my head as these two crazy hotshots approached my tank. They weren't even in any kind of proper uniform. They were wearing olive drab T-shirts with the sleeves cut off, psychedelic bandanas on their heads, and large shiny peace symbols around their necks. They also wore strange looking headsets instead of a normal helmet.

They where laughing and scratching their balls while they checked out our damaged tank. "Looks pretty fucked up," one of them said. The other guy just shook his head, looked up at me, and asked, "Hey man, you guys got any beer?" It was six o'clock in the morning! I knew right then it was going to be a very long day.

Jim handed these two misplaced Hippies a couple of warm beers and all six of us got to work. Since the bad track couldn't be fixed on the spot and since you can't tow a tank with just one, we disconnected both the tracks. In about two hours, we were ready to start our roller-coaster ride down to the bottom of the mountain. You really have to picture this: ninety uncontrollable tons of steel going down a steep mountain with two sections of track hooked to the rear of my tank flying all over the trail knocking down everything in its path!

About halfway down, we lost the two sections of track and Stick was yelling something about not wanting to die. I have to admit that I, too, was more than a little scared. The four of us were crowded together sitting behind those two crazy guys driving the bridge tank. At least, I hoped one of them was driving.

Let me tell you, it wasn't long before we slid around our last sharp turn and started to slow down on the valley floor. I think Stick wanted to jump off and kiss the ground when we finally came to a stop. I just loved that kid! I could see our new home was straight ahead of us.

It was a very small, makeshift compound with just three 105 howitzers, three ammunition carriers, and five armored cavalry assault vehicles. Of course, it was wrapped in barbed wire with all of the normal defensive stuff around. I've passed a hundred of these temporary compounds while in Vietnam, now I was going to live in one.

After my legs stopped shaking, I went to report to the compound's company commander. I checked out our new home as I was looking for the CO. It was rather pretty around here. The valley was real green, the grass wasn't too tall, and you could see a large brown river that was maybe a quarter of a mile away. If it weren't for the war, this would be a perfect place to have a picnic!

I found the captain and he told me a new set of track would be requested and should be here in the morning. He then told me to make ourselves at home and said there was still some breakfast left in the Mermite cans as he pointed in their direction. Hot chow really sounded good to my guys!

It took us two days of hard work to finally get the Double Deuce in proper running order. A lot of the guys from the artillery outfit helped us get the job done even faster than we thought we could. We were starting to get a little spoiled with the two hot meals every day and it was nice making all these new friends. We had worked hard but took time to have some fun, too. Stick and Chris even went down to the river to take a bath.

But it was now time to get back to our own outfit. Before we left, the captain asked me if I would do him a favor and tow a broken down ACAV that needed a new engine across the river for him. It would be picked up in the morning by a maintenance team from their base camp. I said sure and had my guys hook up the tow bar. We left just before noon.

We were soon out of sight of the compound and were driving along the river's edge heading toward the crossing point 300 yards to our front. As we got near to the crossing, I told Chris that since we didn't know how deep it was going to be that he should keep the Deuce floored while crossing. If the water got too deep and went over our exhaust pipes, we could suck water into the engine if he let backed off the gas.

I stopped the tank at the point of crossing and had the crew check out the tow bar again. I didn't want to lose the ACAV in the river. The river looked pretty wide to me, maybe 150 yards or so. It also looked cold and muddy. I told Chris to kick our baby in the ass and get going.

The Deuce leaped forward under our added weight and soon we were cutting our way through the water and getting in pretty deep. The water was splashing into the driver's compartment which meant it was already well over our road wheels! I was thinking, *Is this high tide or what?* Then our tank dropped into a giant hole! I fell forward as I watched our gun tube disappear under the dirty brown river. I yelled for Chris to keep it floored as I felt the Deuce finally land on the bottom of this bomb crater!

The Deuce started to fight its way to the surface. I said out loud to no one in particular, "Thank God we're going to make it," as the ACAV started to drop into the hole. The Deuce was now almost out of danger, but as our tank was picking up speed, the ACAV buried itself against the wall of the crater. I watched in complete horror as the Deuce slowly stopped its forward motion and then plunged back into the muddy water.

I looked inside the turret to see Stick and Jim trying to get out through the loader's hatch. The water was as high as the main gun's breech. Anything that wasn't tied down was floating past my view as I stared in disbelief. *Oh my God, what about Chris?* The driver's compartment was two feet below the breech.

I leaned over the 50-caliber machine gun and looked down in the direction of the driver's area. I could see bubbles coming up to the surface! Chris was still down there with his foot on the gas pedal! I yelled for him to get out of there and seconds later saw him swim to the top. He had the silliest grin on his face!

So here we are sitting in the middle of the river, our engine is full of water, we can't get out, and now I don't even have a working radio to call for help. I'm really in deep shit now! About that time, Chris walked down to the end of our gun tube and with cheers from Stick and Jim, dives into the water! Kids! Why did I get stuck with kids?!

We sat there for three hours until we finally saw an ACAV coming in our direction. They had gotten worried about us when they couldn't reach us on the radio. By sunset, we got word that in the morning an M88 (vehicle track retriever) would be arriving to pull us out and there would also be a new tank to replace our good friend the Double Deuce. We were all sad about that part of the plan as the Deuce had been very special to all of us and had come through for us over and over again. It was like losing a member of the crew.

So here we are, stuck in the middle of the river for the whole, long night just watching the water rise. We sat huddled together on the top of the tank all night. We had no communications or anything. Luckily we didn't have any enemy contact since all we had to fight with was the 50-caliber machine gun. Nothing else worked.

Early the next morning after a long and wet night, the M88 pulled into sight. It would take us all morning to pull everything out of the river and by noon we were again heading down the road in our new tank, the Double Deuce, Jr.! It would take four hours to reach our platoon and during that time I kept thinking, *Nobody will ever believe this story.*

Believe It or Not

The tanks of B company second platoon had already started to set up their night defensive position as I finally decided upon just the right position to park Bravo Two-Two, my new reliable tank. We were once again on a routine and hopefully uneventful search and destroy mission. I picked a location directly under a giant tree as I figured its huge branches would help keep most of the early morning monsoon rain off the tank. As Chris backed us into our new home for the night, I thought, *This is great! We will surely stay dry when that rain hits around two in the morning.* You could almost set your watch by the twice-daily downpour of rain at three in the afternoon and two in the morning.

This section of Vietnam was new to me. I'd never been this close to Laos before. The vegetation seemed so much greener here and the jungle was a lot thicker, too. I'd be glad when we returned to base camp in a few days, but at least we weren't bored by traveling down the same roads all of the time.

I had just finished setting up a poncho over the tank commander's hatch hoping this would also help keep us dry when I heard someone say, "Fuck you!" I knew it wasn't my crew as I could see them busily laying out the barbed wire some fifty feet in front of our tank. I didn't hear it again so I just finished tying down the poncho and soon forgot about it.

About fifteen minutes later as I sat on top of the turret lighting a smoke, I heard it again, "Fuck you, fuck you." This time I stood up and jerked my body around in a circle. There was no one there. *What the hell was going on? Was someone playing tricks or what?* I was starting to get a little upset. As I was looking behind the tank I still couldn't see anyone but there it was again - "Fuck you, fuck you." I was starting to get pissed. I shouted back, "Fuck you too!"

Just about that time, Sergeant First Class Groves, my platoon sergeant, came up to the rear of my tank giving me a stern look asking, "What did you say?"

177

I quickly replied, "Not you, Sarge. Somebody is yelling 'Fuck you' at me!"

He just stood there with his hands on his hips and burst out laughing. After a moment, he said, "That's right, you're new to this part of Vietnam. Don't you know what that is?"

"Hell no, I thought it was you playing a game on me."

"No, Deuce, that's a 'fuck you' lizard. Here, watch this," and he yelled up into the tall, thick trees, "Fuck you, fuck you!" Almost immediately a high-pitched voice called back with a very clear, "Fuck you, fuck you."

"Wow, that's far out!" was all I could say.

I never did get a good close-up look at the big green lizard, he really blended in well with the thick tree limbs. He always had to have the last word, too (just like a woman!). The whole crew had a good time yelling back and forth with our three-foot-long friend. The lizard must have gotten bored with this silly game though as it soon stopped the chatter. But as it was leaving it gave us all one more long and clear, "Fuck youuuuuu." Now that was cool! Ask any Vietnam vet and he'll tell you about those "fuck you" lizards.

Our mission was indeed an uneventful one - except for the lizard, of course. And on the last night not only did we get our evening chow delivered by chopper, but we also a brand spanking new second lieutenant. He was the topic of conversation on our long ride back to Quang-Tri, our base camp the next day.

Lieutenant Roberts was a fresh-faced newly-commissioned twenty-year-old straight from stateside and he was eager to whip us into shape. We'd been there before and had a good idea of the joys that lay ahead. New lieutenants like to do things by the book and it usually took us enlisted men about three weeks to get them around to seeing things our way - the 'Nam way.

Sure enough, two days later we were standing in formation getting our uniforms and boots inspected! Next came tank inventory, weapons inspection, etc. Boy, this was a pain in the ass. However, what came next was even too much for any professional soldier to take. Lt. Roberts wanted to take the second platoon out into the jungle and practice tank tactics! As soon as those unbelievable words were spoken, all us tank commanders looked questionably at SFC Groves. This veteran, thirty-year career soldier with three tours in Vietnam just gave us one of those what-can-I-do looks.

It was the winter of 1970 and most of us tank commanders were on our second or even third tour in the 'Nam and really weren't in the mood for this kind of bullshit, but Groves had just said, "Yes, sir," and told us to get our butts in gear and load up. By 10:00 A.M., all five tanks of the second platoon were driving out of base camp and heading for who knows where.

We drove on the main road for almost an hour until we reached the base of a large mountain. I had been listening to Stick and Jim bitching all the way here. It seemed our young lieutenant had been complaining about the condition of their hooch. Hell, we only lived there for maybe a total of one month out of the whole year, what did he expect?

I was glad when we cut off the main road and started our slow climb up the vast mountain ahead. I hoped this exercise wouldn't take all day, as I didn't really want to be out in the rain at 3:00 P.M. Lt. Roberts was in the lead tank, Bravo Two-One, and upon reaching a rice paddy at the first clearing, he started to cut across its middle. I heard SFC Groves saying over the radio, "Bravo Two-One, this is Bravo Two-Four, don't cross there, you'll sink! Take the outer edge to your left front. Over."

We heard Bravo Two-One say, "Roger Two-Four," as he came to a sudden halt and slowly turned onto the outer edge of the paddy. We all knew you never drove directly across a rice paddy! That was part of Vietnam 101!

Soon we had successfully maneuvered all five tanks around the paddies and now sat lined up looking at a large, flat clearing. Groves told us to take the next thirty minutes as a maintenance break and for the tank commanders to report to his location. It was now around one-thirty in the afternoon and I could smell the monsoon in the air.

As I ran toward Groves' tank, I could see Jim sitting in the tank commander's hatch as Chris and Stick started to check the track tension. Lt. Roberts was all excited as he demonstrated the four basic commands for tank maneuvers: Echelon Left and Right, the sign for a Wedge Formation, and the Column or Straight Line Formation. We all looked at him like he was crazy! Back in the world you could do those maneuvers, but here in the 'Nam there were only two ways to travel, in a column or on line. The jungle made sure of that! But we resigned ourselves to the fact that the lieutenant was an FNG (fucking new guy) and we'd have to play his game no matter what we thought. I went back to my tank and ate C-rations for lunch. My guys laughed when I told them the purpose of the meeting.

Pretty soon, all five tanks were side-by-side on line at the far end of our large open field. The lieutenant was in the middle tank and gave us the charge sign by pointing his hand over his head and then lowering it to his front (it looked like he was passing an invisible football). Now I know what the men under General Custer must have felt like!

A large cloud of smoke bellowed out of each tank as we all started running across the field. I remember yelling, "Charge!" over the intercom when Chris nailed the Double Deuce to the floor. About three minutes later, the platoon leader gave the hand signal for the wedge formation and all the tanks to the left and right of Bravo Two-One dropped back until a perfect inverted V formed. I was actually starting to get into this stuff. It reminded me of my training days at Fort Knox, Kentucky!

I had a real good view from my tank's position at the far right and while not perfect, our small group looked pretty good. About that time, I heard Chris yelling at me that the ground was getting pretty soft and he could feel the Deuce starting to sink. As Chris slowed down, I put in a fast call to Bravo Two-Four (SFC Groves) and informed him the field was getting too soft. I could see his tank also slowing as the lieutenant gave us the charge sign while picking up his own speed. He wasn't even looking back at us when Groves gave the command over the radio for all tanks to stop where they were. The lieutenant must have traveled another forty yards before his tank dropped into a quicksand pit.

Within minutes, Bravo Two-One was buried up to its turret ring (about five feet off the ground)! It was as if the tank had hit a brick wall. We couldn't believe what we were seeing! The loader went flying forward off the tank and landed face first in the soft, muddy field and the lieutenant damn near ate the 50-caliber as he tried to keep from falling. I sat and watched for another five minutes as the tank sank another two feet deeper into the ground. When it was over, only about four feet of the turret was left above the muddy field.

It was now 3:00 P.M. and the monsoon rains were upon us! We tried everything to pull that tank out of the mud and needless to say, everyone out there was covered from head to toe with the muck. Not even hooking up our four remaining tanks in line using tow cables would help. All we could do was call for an M88 (tank recovery vehicle) to come to our aid. It would be hours before that arrived. The new lieutenant put in a call to base camp to inform our CO (company commander) of the situation. All we could do now was sit in the rain and wait.

A short time later, we heard the M88 roaring toward us and I also saw a Huey landing in our small perimeter. It was the CO along with our battalion commander. They started yelling at Lt. Roberts even before he reached their location! *Man, I wouldn't want to be in his boots!*

By now, the only thing you could see was the top two feet of Bravo Two-One. We had removed the machine guns, ammunition, radio, and anything else of value. It was late and even the M88 failed to get the tank out of the mud. The lieutenant rode back in the chopper and SFC Groves led our four remaining mud-covered tanks off the mountain and headed back toward home. The next day, a demolition team was sent to the site. Since we couldn't get the tank out, it would have to be destroyed.

By the time we reached the motor pool back at base camp, everybody within sight was laughing at our platoon for losing an entire tank. And yes, the next few days would be filled with wisecracks about the great adventure of the second platoon.

181

We unloaded everything, topped off our tanks with fuel, and made it back to the company area just in time to see Lt. Roberts departing the area in the back of the company commander's jeep. His footlocker and duffel bag accompanied him. Chris asked me where he was going and all I could say was, "I don't know, but he won't be on a tank, that's for sure!"

I saw him a few months later at his new job, Assistant OIC (Officer in Charge) of the Saigon main PX (post exchange). He told me if I ever needed an icebox or anything to let me know. I wanted to ask him if they made him pay for that tank, but I just didn't have the heart.

Khe Sanh - My Last Battle

Stick and I sat on top of the Double Deuce in the motor pool watching the long column of tracks from the 1/61st Infantry Battalion roll by. We both had bandanas covering our faces because the huge clouds of red dust were bellowing high into the air. It had to cover at least a square mile by now. The whole 5th Infantry Division was on the move. We were going to Khe Sanh and the crew of the Double Deuce was just waiting in line for the word to move out. Nobody ever said anything good about Khe Sanh and it wasn't any different this time. Finally it was our turn, and the tanks of B company joined the already five-mile-long convoy.

I was at Khe Sanh before, in 1968, with the 11th Armored Cavalry Regiment and it was no picnic then. I thought it was going to be a long hard trip for the tanks, and I was right. The deeper we drove into the heart of the steep rocky mountains surrounding Khe Sanh, the narrower and more dangerous the road became. We even had to cross over a narrow gorge between two mountains by using a portable forty-foot span off of a bridge tank that had been wedged between two jagged peaks. Only Chris, my driver, remained in the tank as I ground guided him across. The rest of my crew, Stick and Jim, cheered us on from the far side. I could see the fear in Chris's eyes and let me tell you I was plenty scared, too.

Khe Sanh was an American base in a valley only a few miles from the DMZ (demilitarized zone) to the north and the Ho Chi Min trail to the west in Laos. It had always been a hot spot. The Marines had been there before 1967 and a lot of good men had died trying to defend this valley. Our complete division was there along with other units of infantry and armor making up at least another division in size. There was even a huge mobile shower unit where you went in one side of the tent, took a shower in hot water, and then came out the other side wearing a complete new uniform including boots! This was the first time I ever saw anything like this and was hard for me to believe it was somebody's job to give showers to soldiers in the field!

Once we arrived at Khe Sanh, we spent the next month rotating duties with our sister units. Sometimes we'd pull perimeter guard and other times we'd be out on search and destroy missions. But our main function was to try and support the ground troops by getting high in the mountains where we could react to their needs as they worked in the heavy bush down in the valleys. We had made light contact off and on and hadn't suffered any deaths, but we did have three or four soldiers get wounded.

One night, Sergeant First Class Groves called all the tank commanders together for a meeting. After the normal smoking and joking, he told us we were going into Laos. Lucky us. It had been sort of off limits to American troops, but we were being sent there to recover three of our 155mm howitzers that had been secretly firing into North Vietnam. They had been there to protect our Air Force pilots bombing the North.

Our sister units of tanks and armored personnel carriers had left earlier that morning and we were going in only as a supporting unit to cover their asses. The heat was unbearable and we were awfully hot and sweaty by the time we got to our assigned location, a large open field, late the next day. We still had three hours of maintenance to pull.

It was after dark before we finally ate chow. The entire area where we parked looked like there had been a lot of B-52 strikes as it was pockmarked with huge bomb craters. They must have been dropping their bombs here for at least a month.

We were in what was left of a large valley with a wide, single-lane road running through it and heading north as far as I could see. I later learned that this was part of the infamous Ho Chi Minh trail that I was now standing on. And don't tell anyone, but I think we had now crossed over the line into North Vietnam!

Rumors were flying that one of the infantry units with armored personnel carriers that had left the day before and had gotten their asses kicked, suffered a large amount of casualties, and now the men refused to go back into battle. Their company commander (CO) had even been relieved of duty! I had never heard anything like that before in my two plus years in the 'Nam. At first, I didn't believe it and then some of our younger guys started to brag and say they needed a good tank company to take over and that's why they sent for us. They would see for themselves soon enough. I knew better, but I wasn't about to pop their bubble.

Later on, the lieutenant came by and said he had heard the same rumor. It made no difference, he said, because we would still be going in before daylight and for us to get as much sleep as we could. Stick hadn't been in very many firefights, at least not like we were about to encounter, so I took a little extra time with him that night and the two of us sat around and talked mostly about home.

The next morning before dawn, all five tanks of the second platoon were at the head of the long column. Behind us were ten APCs (what we called ACAVs when I was in the 11th Armored Cavalry Regiment) lined up on the road. The Double Deuce was the second tank in the column.

As the sun broke through the jungle, we heard the sound of outgoing artillery as were started to roll forward. Then the shelling stopped as we saw a low-flying jet drop his load of napalm. We picked up our speed a little and I did a fast check of our guns to make sure they were all switched to the fire position. I told the crew to be alert and get ready as I loaded my own 50-caliber machine gun.

Everything remained very quiet. All you could hear was the clicking of the tracks as they stirred the once calm road into an instant cloud of dust. We went a couple of miles farther down this bomb-ridden road laden with the unmistakable smell of napalm, then the Deuce dropped into a deep ravine and out of sight from the rest of our convoy.

Once we hit bottom, I couldn't even see over the top. I lost sight of Bravo Two-One, the tank that was supposed to be in front of me, and Chris really had to floor it so we could push the fifty-tons of steel up the other side back onto the road. We had no place to build up any speed and even though Chris was flooring it, we were only barely able to crest the top of the ravine. The belly of our tank was now showing! That was not good by any means! It was like asking to get hit in our weakest spot!

Somehow we made it through this hurdle okay and I could see that Bravo Two-One was now far ahead of us. I told Chris to keep his foot to the floor as we accelerated to catch up.

As the Double Deuce moved forward, I quickly scanned the area and saw that the right side was nothing but a series of low rolling hills, maybe five or ten feet tall. It was all open ground and was now smoldering from the napalm which had destroyed any chance for the enemy to hide without being seen. Straight ahead and to our left was a cleared field of short elephant grass running for about one hundred yards before it turned into a wall of thick jungle with bombed trees scattered about. I had a gut feeling that within that jungle and under those fallen trees, the eyes of the enemy were watching us.

We were still moving rather slowly and the tracks behind us were playing catch up. Just before cresting a small rise, I could see a large cloud of billowing dark black smoke straight ahead. Within seconds, we saw two of our own choppers, one Loach and one Huey, still burning on the left side of the road. On the right were two empty APCs and not very far from them lay two burning M48 tanks. The smoke was now so thick that it was hard to tell how much damage had been done. They must have been burning for at least twenty-four hours because the rubber had already melted off the road wheels. Another tank was off in a crater completely turned over on its side. The hull and turret must have had twenty rocket-propelled grenade holes punched through. At that moment, I knew we were going into some kind of real heavy shit! As we moved ahead, I lit a smoke and wished that I had a good strong drink to go with it.

After seeing such a horrifying site, like nothing I had ever seen before, and realizing there were no bodies lying around, it really hit me it must have been a hell of a fight just to get our dead and wounded out of this awful place. Now I started to believe that maybe the rumors were true.

As we slowly worked our way around the burning tanks, I turned my gun tube to the left facing the wood line. Our tanks were about twenty yards apart when all of a sudden I heard a loud explosion.

At first I thought we were getting shot at, then I saw a large cloud of dust and realized that the platoon leader's tank in front of me must have hit a mine. As I wiped the dust from my eyes, a chunk of road wheel went flying past my head.

I bent over to grab my hand mike to call Bravo Two-One and see if they were okay, when BANG! We also hit a 250-pound mine! The Double Deuce flew straight up in the air turning sideways before landing back on the road. The impact of the explosion slammed me down to the turret floor. Stick also really got slammed around, but was now helping me back into the tank commander's hatch. I yelled, "Aim for the tree line, fire!" and instantly heard Jim, my confused gunner, yelling "On the way."

Jim then continued firing with the 30-caliber coax machine gun as Stick humped the heavy main gun rounds as fast as he could. Finally, I crawled back into position and started to fire the 50-caliber as POP, POP, POP our main gun went off. As I reloaded, I looked down into the turret and could see Stick was so busy he had empty round casings everywhere and no time to be scared. Poor Stick, I sure felt sorry for him as I could hear Jim yelling at him to load faster.

In my headphones, I could hear Chris yelling, "What should I do?" All I had time to say was, "Stay down, Chris." I was again busy reloading my 50-caliber and I could hear the RPGs flying over our heads and watched as some of them fell short, exploding in front of our tank. We were putting out so much firepower that I don't think the enemy could get a good shot. I didn't know it then, but all five of the second platoon's tanks had been hit at the same time by command-detonated mines.

In only twenty-five minutes, my outstanding crew had fired every main gun round on the tank, all fifty-four of them! It felt like hours and everything seemed to be happening in slow motion. In reality, we had fired over two rounds a minute including the time it took for us to remove the rounds from our honeycombs! We ran out of 90mm ammunition and had melted the gun barrel on the coax, but I was still laying down protective fire with my 50-caliber as I gave the order to my crew to get out and get behind the tank.

Stick pulled out the radio from the rack and threw it out the loader's hatch onto the ground. We weren't going to leave it for the enemy. After all my guys were off the tank and in a safe place in a large gully on the right side of the road, I pulled the butterfly handle off the 50-caliber and jumped down. We felt like ducks out of water as we huddled behind our blown-up tank. All of a sudden, we became infantrymen with only two rifles and one 45-caliber pistol between the four of us.

Out of nowhere, two APCs pulled up behind us and were laying down cover fire with their M60 machine guns, but they were too far away for us to get there safely. Instead, I crawled forward about twenty meters to check on the platoon leader and his crew. They were also huddled behind their tank. The lieutenant had been wounded in the arm and his driver was dead, but the gunner was still okay.

More friendly artillery started to impact close around us, I mean real close, and the enemy fire turned into just random spurts. One of the two APCs that had tried to help took a direct hit so they loaded the wounded on the other track and moved back toward the rear of the column. Soon we could hear an M-88 (vehicle recover track or VTR) as it pulled up to my location and their crew started to hook us up for towing. At that time, all the remaining tank crews came to my tank and we loaded up everybody on the VTR and started to get the hell out of there! Everyone was firing into the wood line as we slowly started to move back towards safety.

I was busy talking to the VTR commander who I'd realized I'd known back in the states. Everybody on board was still firing their rifles as we were starting to again receive increased enemy fire. Then it happened. I watched as three more rockets slowly came flying toward us from the direction of the wood line. One hit in front of our VTR, the second one hit the right front idler arm of my tank, and the last one was a direct hit on my brand new ill-gotten Mermite can! Now I was pissed! Not to mention I got wounded on my hand by the scrap metal (I didn't even know that until later that night).

It took us an hour to get towed back to the safety of our own perimeter. Out of the five tanks, mine was the only one left that had enough good parts and could safely be towed back in. Now I knew how the guys must have felt yesterday.

Once we returned to our own company area, I finally felt safe and was glad this battle was over for us. At least, I thought it was. We were totally soaked and both physically and emotionally exhausted. All we wanted to do was find something cold to drink and sleep. But a short time later, this heavyset warrant officer came up to me and told his mechanics to look at my tank. He was smoking a big cigar and informed me he had plenty of used parts for me and pointed with his big cigar in the direction of a nearby bomb crater full of destroyed tanks and APCs.

He must have seen the disbelief in my eyes as he said, "Parts, son, I got lots of parts," and laughingly told my crew and me to go get some chow as his people would have our tank back together in about four hours. Boy, the chief must really want me back in the battle. Just my luck!

That evening as I was getting the metal RPG fragments pulled out of my hand, some general landed and said we did a good job and that each man would get two beers with his dinner tonight. About the same time as the general was saying that to the troops, my guys, Chris and Stick, were busy appropriating a case of beer off the chopper pad!

We were sitting around talking when a pretty French female news reporter and her two cameramen came up and asked us what it had been like out there. We were too tired and too busy trying to see her tits to worry about what she was saying, but some young soldier came running up looking like it was his first firefight or something and said, "It was hell! You can call it the road of no return." He was so serious that we all had to bust out laughing! I felt like telling the girl that she could ride with me in the morning, but I didn't.

At dawn the next day, I was sitting on the turret of my tank (with a hangover). I knew I was to be the lead and only tank in the column with two APCs behind me then two trucks with quad 50-

189

calibers and six more APCs behind them. Some major came up to me and said I had ten minutes before we took off. I dropped down in my turret and located my hidden bottle of Crown Royal, took a good drink and passed it down to my crew. Even Stick took a swig.

As my guys took a drink I said, "Well, guys I don't think we're going to make it out of this one."

At the same time we were looking at each other, smiling, and said, "Ain't no big thing." Stick added, "What will they do if we don't go? Send us to Vietnam?" We all laughed and five minutes later we were on the move.

This time we knew what to expect. We slowly moved forward and as we came over the steep crest on the other side of the ravine, I could now see where we had been hit yesterday. As I started firing main gun rounds and the quad 50-calibers opened up behind me, my stomach was tied up in knots. I was just waiting to get hit! I knew it would be just a matter of time. Then a call came over the radio, "Stop where you are. I repeat, stop where you are." Chris slammed on the brakes before I could even tell him to. "The mission is canceled. Return to our location!" said the wonderful voice at the other end of the radio.

All I could think about was turning the big ol' Double Deuce around and hauling ass out of there, but instead I played it by the book. I took up a defensive position while the rest of the convoy turned around and then I followed behind with my gun tube facing the rear. At the last minute, higher command decided to blow the artillery guns rather than lose any more men and equipment. I can remember thinking, *Boy this has to be the luckiest day of my life!* Within thirty days, I would be on a plane going home. I had just fought my last fight!

Chris Cordova My Friend

I really felt lucky to have such a good crew, even if their backgrounds were so different. Jim was from New York and had a college degree. Stick was the skinny kid from Detroit who had been raised in the streets of the Motor City and then there was Chris who was a small town kid who had never ventured far beyond the beautiful mesas of New Mexico. As a tank commander, I felt blessed when these three men were filtered down through the system and finally ended up being assigned to my tank. Jim was the anchor of my crew while Chris was the hardest worker. Stick was just Stick. Always a little nervous, but at the same time eager to learn the art of war and always doing a good job for me. When these three guys bonded together I knew that the crew of Bravo Two-Two was going to be a good one! We had become an unbeatable team.

I knew Chris Cordova, the driver of our tank, for almost a year. He arrived in Vietnam when he was nineteen and we had a party when he turned twenty. We had a lot of good times together along with a few bad ones. His best friend and running buddy was Jim Tanouse, our gunner on the Double Deuce. They were always doing something together. Chris was a young, quiet Mexican-American boy and Jim at the age of twenty-three was the older teacher. They both had been drafted so they shared that common bond. I can remember Chris always going to church services as often as he could, even while we were in the field. There might have been only two soldiers at the services, but one of them was always Chris. I had managed to take good care of my guys for the whole year that I was their tank commander.

Chris had extended for six months in Vietnam so that when he got home he would have no duties to perform in the National Guard. People who were drafted not only had to go to Vietnam, but they also had to serve with the National Guard for a year or two, I don't remember exactly how long. This program was new and a lot of the guys were doing it. It meant that Chris would now be leaving the 'Nam four months after me.

I was busy in base camp starting the week-long ordeal of out-processing to go home, Jim was out of country on R&R in Australia and our platoon was preparing to leave Quang-Tri on another support mission. As usual, Chris was driving the old Double Deuce, Stick was the loader, and our newly assigned second lieutenant would be acting as tank commander for this mission. The five tanks of the second platoon, B company would be on a search and destroy mission around Alpha Four, our furthermost fire support base which was north of Quang Tri. They would be supporting our sister unit, the 1/61st Infantry Battalion.

I was later told that they had made contact with a platoon of North Vietnamese Army soldiers. The American soldiers from the 1/61st in their ACAVs had the enemy pinned down in a valley while our tanks blocked the exits so they couldn't escape. Soon our ACAVs started taking heavy return fire and had to back out of the area while at the same time calling in our gunships for support. Shortly, there were three Cobra gunships circling the area.

The gunships started their attack by coming in low from the north firing their machine guns until they were on their final approach toward the enemy infested pod of jungle that was buried within the heart of the valley. Then they fired a series of rockets toward the target area as the crews of the second platoon watched from a safe distance. The tankers cheered as the exploding rockets found their mark. But then it happened! For no apparent reason, the third gunship made his run from the east end of the valley and headed straight in the direction of our own tanks sitting one hundred yards above the target area! The Cobra fired off two rockets, the first one landing twenty feet directly in front of the Double Deuce. Our new lieutenant, who had only seconds before been sitting on the right front fender talking with Chris and Doc Brown, our medic, was blown completely off the tank! Doc had also been hit by the first rocket and was now lying on the ground seriously wounded.

About the same time, the second rocket found its mark. It exploded upon impact and penetrated the hull of the Double Deuce. It landed directly above Chris's head and my good friend was killed instantly. Within moments of the second explosion, Stick was already climbing out of the turret and heading in the direction of his buddy but by the time he got there, it was too late. All that Stick could do was to sit next to Chris and cry. He was still crying when the other troopers of the second platoon finally reached them. The lieutenant would recover from his wounds, but Doc would later lose his left arm due to this terrible tragedy.

For me, this was the worst day of my life. I had lost a very special friend and I still to this day feel that if only I had been there, things might have been different. An investigation was launched to determine why or how such a terrible mistake had happened.

I went to the motor pool that afternoon to clean the blood of my friend off my tank. I couldn't and wouldn't let anybody help. I was the tank commander of the Double Deuce and it was my job, my responsibility.

It took me over two hours to scrub down the entire driver's compartment. I still remember that I didn't want anyone to see my tears as I tried to erase the memories of what had just happened. Maybe if I scrubbed hard enough, Chris would be all right. I'd never before or since cried so hard. There was to be none of the normal joking going around the motor pool on this day. Everybody knew and liked Chris.

Two days later, I had to tell Jim when he returned from R&R. It was so hard to explain what had happened to his best buddy. We both sat in the dark corner of our hooch and cried together. I didn't think I had any tears left. The next morning, I sat down and wrote a letter to Chris Cordova's parents while at the same time promising myself never to forget him. I even made a vow that I would name my next son after him.

Many years later in 1990, my second wife, Sue, and I had the first of two very special sons and we named him Christopher. I had finally been able to keep my promise from so long ago. Christopher, as well as our second son, Billy, was born with a rare, terminal metabolic disorder called Leigh's Disease. When little Chris was only three weeks old, he stopped breathing while he was lying in front of me on the floor! I was busy watching TV at the time and was very surprised at what happened next. I could see my old friend Chris standing next to the television and pointing in the direction of my son! I was startled to say the least, but I immediately looked down to see my boy turning blue. I then gave little Chris CPR and he came around just fine.

While I was busy performing CPR I realized that my son had a guardian angel. My dear friend of so long ago had just alerted and helped me save Christopher's life. My friend Chris may be gone but he will never be forgotten. When it's my turn to enter Fiddlers' Green, the final resting place for all good tankers, I know my good friend Chris will be waiting for me. He'll be standing there with that shit-eating grin and laughing that boyish laugh. We'll both climb onboard the gleaming Double Deuce and I'll holler out, "Kick her in the ass, Chris, we have a long way to go before it gets dark." As the Deuce heads out into the clouds, a fellow trooper will shout, "Hey, guys, look at that crazy chicken on the gun tube!"

Many years later while standing on top of a wind-swept mesa in New Mexico, I would visit my friend again.

Last Flight Out

The bonding of men. That's only four words, but how do I explain them to you? It's not like being a member of a football team in high school or like the closeness of college fraternity brothers. It's so much more than that. Soldiers belong to a unique brotherhood of war. We share a proud heritage left by those who served with honor and dignity. We share a special camaraderie unique to those who enjoyed the best of times together and survived the very worst. A bond so strong that you wouldn't think twice about sacrificing your life to save a fellow soldier. I think that special bond is our reward for doing what we knew was right, even though some thought it was wrong.

Many times a soldier's normal day would be your worst and our worst day is kept buried deep inside our souls only to be shared, if at all, among fellow soldiers. It can't easily be talked about with our civilian friends or family, no matter how close. I know, I've tried. That goes for the family and friends who lost loved ones in Vietnam. They, too, find it hard to share their hurt and loneliness. To those families, I want you to know there are many of us who knew your sons and share in your great loss and in whose memories they will remain forever.

One cannot hope to share the full experience of war. It can't be shown in movies or written about in a book. Each soldier keeps part of it within himself and it can't be automatically retrieved. It's our proud burden to keep and hold until, God forbid, another war. Then there will be more young men who will understand the meaning of the words pride, honor, comradeship, and esprit de corps. They will then understand that lasting bond between men in time of war.

It was May 10, 1971. I was twenty-five-years old and had been fighting for almost three years. The war in Vietnam was finally over for me and I was going home for good. The death of my dear friend, Chris, had taken the last of the fight out of me. The wounds on my body had healed, but the ones inside would take years longer.

This time, I was ready to go home, more determined to adjust to life in the world.

Proudly, I boarded the freedom bird for the last time. Even if the United States was divided by the war, I had the satisfaction of knowing I had done my best. I had fought in nine of the eleven major campaigns of the war and had a chest full of medal to prove it.

The one award of which I am most proud, even more so than my Bronze Stars and Purple Hearts, is my Combat Infantrymen's Badge (CIB). I earned that award while I was in the ARPs and it was the toughest to achieve. I would, however, trade all my ribbons if only I could have Chris back again.

As the freedom bird lifted off the runway, the stewardess gleefully yelled out, "Up, up and away. Next stop the world!" I thought to myself, *Yeah, I've heard that before.*

Section Five
Closing the Doors

♦   Going to See Chris
♦   Closing the Door For Frank
♦   My Buddy Kenny

Going to See Chris

I'm writing this story in memory of my friend Chris Cordova and for all of us who were privileged to have known him during his short life. It's three o'clock in the morning, Friday July 3, 1998. I just opened the garage door of my home in Las Vegas and I'm on my way back into the house to get my coffee. I can hear the deep mellow sound of the dual exhaust on my restored classic, a 1960 Chevy El Camino, echoing off the garage walls. I'm going to visit the final resting place of Chris Cordova with whom I served some twenty-eight years ago in Vietnam.

After many hours of research with the help of my wife, Sue, we were able to locate Chris's hometown and with Sue's magic fingers on the keyboard of the computer, we even had a phone number for Robert Cordova who turned out to be the younger brother of Chris! After talking with Robert and finding out exactly were Mosquero, New Mexico, was, I decided that I needed to go and say a final goodbye to my young friend. I needed to close that door as I opened some new ones. Some 750 miles and fourteen hours from now, I'll finally be with my friend again.

The traffic was light as I drove over Hoover Dam, navigated the steep canyon, and headed for Kingman, Arizona. The trip was nice and it stayed cool all the way to Flagstaff before I rolled down the windows to pick up a breeze. I love driving across I-40. Being a classic car buff, I really enjoy going seventy-miles-per-hour and looking into the backyards along the way to see what kind of old cars were parked there. On this trip, I didn't hear the normal, "Stop looking around and keep your eyes on the road," that Sue would constantly be telling me. This journey was on my own. This was my quest, something I had wanted to do for a long time.

Around three o'clock that afternoon, I pulled into Tucumcari, New Mexico, and started on Route 54 toward the town of Logan. It was nice to get off the interstate and travel on the back roads again. The weather was great! Hot, but still very nice with white clouds cutting off the heat of the sun every so often. When I arrived in Logan, I followed the old Main Street through the city. You could see that at one time it must have been a busy place, but now a lot of the stores were closed and boarded, just as in many small towns across the country.

As I kept going north, the road seemed to be getting smaller and smaller until I finally turned on Route 39 and headed the tiny town of Mosquero, my final destination. Now the road was a narrow, two-lane highway that seemed to be darting out into nowhere. There were nothing but green rolling hills all around with only a few ranch houses scattered about to interrupt this gorgeous land.

By now, I was starting to get really nervous. I kept thinking about all the things that I wanted to say to Chris. And I was also nervous about meeting the Cordova family. Did they want to meet me? Had they put everything in the past or would they want me to tell them everything I remembered from all those years ago? I guess I really didn't know what to expect.

After going about twenty miles, I approached the base of a beautiful mesa. I was sure it would drop off toward the right side and go into a valley where Mosquero would be found but instead, as I reached a fork in the road, I started to climb right up the side. It was very steep and I was just hoping my old car would make it up through the steep sharp curves.

As I slowly maneuvered my way through this wonderful mesa, I came upon a huge wall of rock and saw it was covered from top to bottom with names and dates. I wondered if Chris had put his name there when he was a boy. Finally reaching the top, I saw nothing but hills covered with juniper trees about as far as you could see. It was nothing like I had expected the top of a mesa to be. I thought it would be flat and rocky. I was hoping there would be a gas station in Mosquero as I was down to a quarter of a tank and still had to travel the thirty miles back to Logan later in the day.

I soon approached the town of Mosquero and luckily saw a gas pump on the right side of town with a big sign reading, "Open" leaning against it. As I pulled toward the old-fashioned gas pump, I couldn't help but think, *Why would anybody want to live in this little spot in the road?* I stopped my car. As I started to get out, an older man approached and asked how I was doing. I returned the greeting as he was removing the front cover on the pump so he could reset the meter by hand (he told me the old pump had broken three years earlier). I asked him if he could answer a couple of questions for me.

First I asked him where the cemetery was located and then I asked if he knew where Robert Cordova lived. "Oh sure, that's easy," he replied and offered to call Chris Cordova (Robert's son who had been named after my friend). Chris Cordova was the local marshal and was usually around.

As he was filling my tank, I was looking over the town. I could see a volunteer fire department building with a "Closed" sign in the window and next to it was a small market with an even smaller bar attached to the side of it and the town's post office. That was downtown Mosquero, New Mexico.

A few minutes later, a pickup truck pulled into the station and a young man walked up to me. I assumed it was Chris and put my hand out to introduce myself, "Hi, I'm Jack. You must be Chris."

"Yes, and I would be happy to take you to the cemetery as soon as you get your gas, sir."

A few minutes later, I was following him down the dusty road to the cemetery. We had only gone a short way before we turned off on a gravel road. Soon my car was covered in a great cloud of white dust. I remember being upset about this and at the same time feeling a little ashamed of myself. Here I was about to see my friend, Chris, and I was worried about a little dust. That was really stupid.

It wasn't long before we were pulling into the small cemetery. It was on about a quarter-acre of land with a fence around it. I guessed there were about thirty graves altogether. I was really nervous now. There were so many things I had wanted to tell Chris.

As we approached the first grave, I could see a headstone engraved: "PFC Jose Cordova Died In Germany World War II." That was the grave of Chris's father who had been killed in action in 1945. I got a lump in my throat. All of a sudden I thought, *His dad was also here and taking care of him. That meant Chris would be all right.*

Then came the real hard part. I walked up to Chris's grave. There was a small stone just like his dad's. It had his name, rank, and where and when he died. There was a small American flag made of flowers in front of the headstone, but the flowers had long since wilted. But you could tell Chris was remembered and not forgotten. His nephew put his hand down and moved the wreath so I could see the complete marker.

As I knelt down, something very strange happened. It was as if Chris had heard all my thoughts about him during the last decade and I really didn't have to say anything because he already knew. With tears in my eyes, all I could say was, "It's good to see you again, old buddy."

I sat there touching the headstone for about five minutes as Chris's nephew backed away to give me some privacy. Finally, I said one more time, "It's good to see you, Chris," and I stood up and walked a few steps backward still looking at the grave. I really felt a sense of peace as I turned and walked back to my car, wiping the tears from my eyes. I didn't want to break down and cry since I still had to meet the rest of his family in a few minutes. The tears would come later when I was alone driving out of Mosquero.

Shortly we were pulling into the Robert Cordova's front yard. His was a large wooden house with new and old cars scattered through the yard. Robert walked out to meet us. For just a moment, I thought it was Chris, they looked so much alike. We shook hands and I could tell this was as awkward for him as it was for me. He introduced me to his sister and then his wife, Francis, and their oldest son, Floyd. I was then invited into their home and offered a beer that I gladly accepted. I'm not really much of a beer drinker any more, but it was really appreciated!

We all sat around in the living room making small talk and I was trying to figure out how to give them a copy of the story I had written about Chris. I decided to pull it out of my pocket and handed it to Robert. I watched as he took the two-page story out of the white envelope. I was scared at that moment. I took another large gulp of beer while wondering if they would like my story or not. *How would they act? Did I do the right thing?* I just waited. The story was passed from one member of the family to the next with only a few nods of their heads as any sign of what they read. I could see Robert's eyes were a little red but other than that, not a word was spoken.

I was offered another beer and after some prodding, accepted a plate of homemade enchiladas. While were all sitting around the table, Robert's daughter-in-law entered the kitchen. "That was a really nice story you wrote about Chris," she said. "We all liked it very much." That was all that was ever said about it, but it did make me feel much better and a little more at ease.

After I had eaten a few more bites of dinner, out came the photo albums. There were lots of pictures in various sizes already in the living room with a separate special area for each one of the sons and cousins who had served in the military. Chris had his spot with his medals hanging next to his basic training picture and next to him was Robert's son, Floyd. Floyd had served in the Persian Gulf, but was now on disability from a back injury.

After a couple of beers, things started to get better. The family shared stories about the two brothers, Chris and Robert, as we sat in this small room on the top of this beautiful mesa in New Mexico. Robert told me about a doctor who also had lost a son in Vietnam and who had built a memorial and chapel in the little town of Angel Fire, eighty miles northwest of Mosquero. All the boys from the surrounding four counties who had died in Vietnam had their pictures and some personal effects placed in the memorial building. Chris's picture, along with his dog tags, were there. Every week a different picture was placed in the chapel and that family was notified. Robert called this place "holy ground." A lot of the conversation was centered on the brothers and how their Uncle Joe had taught them to swim in the local swimming hole, to hunt, and to fish.

Soon, with a third beer in our hands, Robert, Floyd, and I headed out the door and on our way "cruzin," as Robert put it. I was no longer a stranger. I had been accepted as a friend. There couldn't have been more than thirty houses in this small town. Many of them had been boarded up as the people who had lived there were now long gone. I was told that when Chris was a boy, there were probably 300 people living in town, but the population had now dwindled to around a hundred. Three of the largest ranchers in the area had bought out most of the small ranches.

As we left the house, we went about a half block away and saw the small, white buildings that were the elementary and high schools. Robert told me a picture honoring Chris was in the main hallway of the high school. We then drove by a church and the little hospital that had closed over ten years ago and was now the school superintendent's house.

Every time we drove past a house, everybody would wave and I would wave back. I could imagine what they must have thought at the site of this strange gringo riding around in Robert's green pickup truck! Everybody knew everyone else in this town. It was like one huge family. You just couldn't help but fall in love with Mosquero.

Robert drove us down Bell Ranch Road for about forty miles. As we drove, more stories came out about Chris's funeral and how Robert was on his senior class fieldtrip to the Lake of the Ozarks when he was notified of brother's death. The class, all five of them, cut the trip short and returned home. He said the whole town turned out for Chris's funeral, as well as the honor guard from the Air Force National Guard in Clovis.

Robert told me about the wild elks that roamed the area and Floyd directed my attention to the local sights such as the Indian caves. When we got to the end of the mesa, they pointed to an area across the valley where dinosaur footprints had been discovered. We had a really nice talk as we returned to their home and I felt I now knew more about Chris than I had known during that whole year we served together.

Robert wanted me to spend the night and kept asking me over and over again, but I didn't feel right about staying. I didn't want to ruin their Fourth of July weekend. Deep inside, I really liked these new-found friends and could easily have stayed longer, but I knew I had to get home to my own little family. It took me nearly thirty years, but I finally was able to close the door on Chris. But I also knew it could be opened again and his family and friends would welcome me.

I departed at dark and as I was driving out of town, the full impact of what had happened hit me. I had to wipe the tears away as I drove off the mesa and headed for the busy world below. I couldn't help but think of the past and how my wife encouraged me to write this book about the way Vietnam really was. About good men doing an impossible job as best they could. Not killers, but boys who became men long before their time - some who came home and some, like Chris, who didn't.

When I wanted and needed to go see Chris, my wife told me, "Go do what you have to do." Sometimes, I think she must understand me better than I understand myself. Thank you, Sue, for helping me close those doors.

Closing the Door for Frank

I just got off the phone with Fran Fleming, Frank Saracino's sister. I had known Frank for less than a month while I was in the ARPs (Aero Rifle Platoon) in 1969. I was his roommate and was with him the day he died.

Fran had been desperately looking for someone to talk to about her brother for more than twenty-nine years. She wanted to know how he died. She wanted to talk to someone who knew or worked with him in Vietnam. She was only a little girl in 1969 and was now determined to put the unknown to rest. But it had been so long and she was close to giving up the search when somehow the name of my friend, Bruce Stephen, was given to her. Bruce and I had served together in the ARPs.

When Bruce called and asked if I would talk to the Saracinos, I told him of course. Until the call came through, I had an uneasy feeling. Questions raced through my mind, *How would I react? Was I really ready for this?* I was expecting to talk to Frank's dad, but it was Fran who made the call. She wanted to screen the information for her distraught father. That was fine with me.

At times, it was hard for me as well as for Fran. It did bring back memories, but the hardest part was trying to explain everything in a way so as not to upset her. Questions about how he died were hard enough to answer, but why he died was almost impossible to explain. How can you explain to someone who wasn't there all the feelings one felt. Like the pride of being in an elite unit, the willingness to give your life for your fellow soldier, or the unselfish risks you would take to help a man you hardly knew?

As we were talking, I got lost in time and my mind took me back to that morning. I was twenty-two and in Vietnam again.

Frank felt just like I did, both scared and excited. This was to be our first combat mission in the ARPs and we had no idea what to expect. The weather was nice, at least it wasn't raining. We flew out to the landing zone in separate choppers as we were in two

207

different squads, but I do remember waving goodbye to Frank as we walked toward our choppers on the heli-pads and saying, "See ya later, buddy." That was the last time I ever heard Frank's laugh.

Was he in a good mood? Yes, I believe he was. He was happy because he had made the team. He was an ARP. He didn't have to, but rather he wanted to be with this outfit, just like the rest of us. Was he scared? Yes, we all were. That, too, was part of the job.

The hardest part of this conversation for me was realizing all of the questions his family still had. Questions that had gone unanswered for such a very long time. I was counting on her asking "how did he die," but not the "was he happy or what was the weather like" questions. "Was he wearing a helmet" or "was he put in a body bag" were a few more questions that caught me off guard. Yes he was wearing a helmet, even though it was optional at the time. Fran asked why didn't the helmet protect him from the bullet and I had to explain that a 51-caliber bullet goes through a helmet like a hot knife through butter. Even while I was saying the words I knew it was hard for her to hear them, but there was no other way to explain it. It was nothing Frank did wrong! He made no mistakes. One bullet in the head and it was all over. At least there was no pain. Maybe now for his family, but not for Frank. For a soldier it was the fastest way to go. I know that might sound strange but it's true. We soldiers actually sat around talking about such things. Death was a very real part of our lives.

Her phone call that Sunday morning made me realize more than anything else that without being able to close the doors, the families of our fallen comrades face Vietnam and what it did to them almost daily. It almost makes me feel guilty for serving in the war and coming home. I only wish I could answer those many questions for all of the friends and families of our fallen comrades. I know what it's like to be able to finally close a door and I know what it feels like to have that weight lifted off your shoulders. Fran, I hope our talk helped. Frank Saracino has a lot of friends like myself and we won't forget him.

After I hung up the phone, my wife Sue asked me if I was all right or would I have nightmares again tonight. Yes, I'll survive this, I always do. But sometimes I do wonder if people really understand the burden we soldiers will always carry, even for many years after our job is done and we are pretending to be normal beings.

My Buddy Kenny

Kenny Orton and I had lived in the small summer resort town of Guerneville, California, on the Russian River seventy miles north of San Francisco. We weren't real close friends like my buddy, George, and I were but we always seemed to be hanging around with the same crowd of kids. Kenny was raised around Guerneville but I'd only lived there during seventh, eighth, and ninth grades. We had moved there shortly before Dad retired from the Army. He had been stationed at Fort Mason in San Francisco.

Kenny, George, Jessy, Steve, and I were the local terrors of the seventh grade. We all hung out together and would do so for the next few years. One good thing about living in a place like Guerneville was there was always something to do and ways to get into trouble! The bad thing, however, was that everybody always found out when you did something wrong. You couldn't get away with anything in that small town!

Kenny was a short, skinny kid who was pretty much a follower. If a group of kids were hanging around, Kenny would always be there but he'd be standing back just a little. He was never the kid in charge. Kenny's father owned Roland's Beach, a small section of sandy beach located on the Russian River directly across the street from my house. That's where I met Kenny in the summer of 1961. I knew some local girls who worked in the snack shack at Roland's Beach and I'd spend a lot of my time there trying to act cool. Kenny was always running up and down the beach yelling and complaining about having to load little kids into the paddleboats his father rented or about having to unload supplies at the snack bar. He just wanted to hang around the girls who visited his father's beach. Work was the last thing on his mind!

It was a known fact that Kenny was always about one step away from getting into trouble. (I was usually only one step behind that!) While in the eighth grade, Kenny, Steve, and I got caught borrowing our elementary school's pickup truck. They always left the keys in it so we would take it out for a joy ride on the many

211

back roads around town. We got away with this for many a Friday night until one time we forgot to turn off the headlights. By Monday morning, the battery was dead! To this day, I don't know how we got caught but by ten in the morning, we were all standing in front of the principal. Punishment was swift in those days. Within the hour, we were all bending over holding our ankles as the giant, wooden paddle with the holes in it rang out in the name of justice!

Freshman year found us at Analy High School in Sepastopol, twenty-seven miles from Guerneville. Kenny would always show up at my door looking for a ride to school. It wasn't cool to ride the bus. Kenny never had his own car, but could always be found sitting in the back seat of someone else's. Every morning it would always be the same. Kenny would start with, "Where are we going today?" Not, "Let's go to school," or "Hurry up, we'll be late!" It was true, most of the time and for sure on Fridays, my old blue 1951 Ford (it had "Mr. Blue" written on each front fender) just couldn't seem to head in the direction of Analy High. Instead, it headed toward the ocean, fifty miles in the other direction, stopping in Guerneville only long enough to pick up more kids. That was the Kenny Orton that I knew.

I left high school in 1963 during my junior year. I was so excited about joining the Army, I don't even think I said goodbye to Kenny. The next time I saw Kenny was in the summer of 1969. I was standing in the motor pool in a place called Xuan Loc in a strange country called Vietnam. I was watching my crew changing a worn-out road wheel on our tank when I heard, "Jack? Jack Stoddard, is that you?"

I turned around to see a young, skinny soldier who was about three inches taller than me. I knew that smile! My mind searched all the faces from my past. Then it clicked! "Kenny, you old son of a bitch! What are you doing here?" It was great to see him. I couldn't even remember the last time I'd ran into anybody from home. And to find an old friend in Vietnam was twice as nice.

After work, we spent most of the night drinking beer and talking about the good old days on the Russian River. Kenny updated me on the happenings of all our friends. It seemed like most of them were in college trying to avoid the draft. That kind of upset me, but at least my friend Kenny was in the Army. It felt great that he was here with me. We spent a lot of time together and soon became even closer then we had been back in the world. I think the 'Nam had a way of doing that.

We were in different units, me as a tanker and Kenny working in the Chemical Corp. His job was to help purify the drinking water for our whole base camp. Kenny wanted to be a combat soldier like me, but I told him his job was even more important then mine. A lot of men counted on that water and without it we couldn't do our jobs. I joined the ARPs about three months later. Kenny also tried, but his commander wouldn't let him go from his unit. It really upset Kenny as he wanted nothing less than to get into the action. He still wanted to become a combat soldier! He wanted that first firefight.

We still remained good friends and would get together about once a month. I was now stationed out of Bien Hoa and Kenny was still at Xuan Loc. Six months later, I would leave Vietnam and once again I didn't get to say goodbye to my old friend. It was December 1969. Merry Christmas, Kenny. A soldier like me didn't last long back in the world and by March 1970 I was once again riding a tank through the rice fields of Vietnam. This time I was way up north in a place called Quang-Tri.

About halfway into my second tour, our unit was working around Khe Sanh. Just holding onto this piece of land had a reputation of being hard and dangerous work. My crew and I were just about worn out from the long hours, lack of sleep, and constant off and on contact with the enemy. It had been a really long two weeks and we'd just pulled back into the base camp and parked the Double Deuce next to the shower point. I was in the process of getting my shaving kit from the bussel rack of the tank when I heard, "Jack? Jack Stoddard, is that you?"

Right away I recognized the voice and turned around expecting to see the same old friend I'd left in Xuan Loc nine months earlier. What I saw sort of looked liked Kenny only much older, tired, and scared looking! I was taken aback by my friend's appearance but I still managed to jump off of my tank and give this "stranger" a big and long hug. My long-awaited hot shower no longer seemed important to me. I yelled up to Jim, my gunner, to throw us down two cold beers from our Mermite can.

Kenny and I sat on a large boulder and sipped our beers in silence for what seemed like an eternity. Then Kenny started to speak. He explained that he had finally become a combat soldier. He also had extended in Vietnam and had volunteered for sniper school. You could hear the excitement in his voice as he slowly started to sound like the Kenny I had always known. He told me all about the special weapons he so proudly carried and the training he had gone through. Then he started to shake and turn away from me as he started to tell me his terrible story.

My dear friend had just returned from the worst mission in his life. I really don't want to tell you his story. I can't, not even today. But what I can tell you is that four snipers had left Khe Sanh the night before and early this morning only Kenny had walked back in. He was now crying and asking for my advice on what he should do next. Should he quit or go back out? I took a long drink from my now warm beer. I told him if it was me, I'd have to go back out at least one more time. Kenny just sat there nodding his head in agreement. We talked for a while longer but I could see that my friend was far away in a different place and time. Soon Kenny, without saying a word, stood up, gave me a long hug, and walked away. I never saw or heard from him again.

In 1998, while doing research for my book, I found the phone number of my friend, George, and decided to call and he answered. After a while, the conversation turned to Kenny. George said that Kenny had called him the year before around Christmas time and told him he'd made it home from Vietnam and graduated from college four years later. He'd become a successful design engineer. George said everything was going well for Kenny until he started getting flashbacks of Vietnam and then everything fell apart. He had become an alcoholic and lost his job, home, and money. George thinks Kenny lives with his parents somewhere in

California. He wouldn't leave his address or phone number with George.

I miss that skinny kid, even if he did manage to keep me in constant trouble! I'd give anything if it could be the way it used to be. Kenny and I skipping school, laughing and telling jokes as old Mr. Blue carried us off to the ocean.

The total number of U.S. Army tankers (enlisted men with MOS 11E10, 11E20, 11E40 and officers with MOS 1203) killed in the Republic of Vietnam were 725.

To put this in perspective it must be understood that only 2,720 men served as tankers in Vietnam from 1966 to 1971. This represents a loss rate of 27%, the highest loss-rate for any MOS in any branch of the military during the war.

I hope you enjoyed reading my book as much as I enjoyed writing it. Vietnam wasn't the same for every man who fought there. This was my Vietnam. This was a story that I had to tell and I hope you found it interesting and maybe learned something new about the war and the soldiers who fought it with pride, honor and dignity.